NX8.5 Tutorial Book
John G. Ronald

This book may not be duplicated in any way without the express written consent of the publisher, except in the form of brief excerpts or quotations for the purpose of review. The information contained herein is for the personal use of the reader and may not be incorporated in any commercial programs, other books, database, or any kind of software without written consent of the publisher. Making copies of this book or any portion for purpose other than your own is a violation of copyright laws.

Limit of Liability/Disclaimer of Warranty:
The author and publisher make no representations or warranties with respect to the accuracy or completeness of the contents of this work and specifically disclaim all warranties, including without limitation warranties of fitness for a particular purpose. The advice and strategies contained herein may not be suitable for every situation. Neither the publisher nor the author shall be liable for damages arising here from.

Trademarks:
All brand names and product names used in this book are trademarks, registered trademarks, or trade names of their respective holders. The author and publisher is not associated with any product or vendor mentioned in this book.

Copyright © 2012 John G. Ronald
All rights reserved.

ISBN-13: 978-1481928762

ISBN-10: 1481928767

Table of Contents

Cover
Title Page
Table of Contents
Introduction

Chapter 1: Getting Started

NX Terminology
Starting a new file
User Interface
Mouse Functions
Color Settings
Shortcut keys

Chapter 2: Basic Part Modeling

Creating Sketches
Adding Constraints and Dimensions to sketches
Creating Extrude Features
Creating Revolved Features
Creating Cut Features
Adding Edge Blends
Creating Drafts
Saving the File

Chapter 3: Creating Assemblies

Starting a new Assembly file
Inserting Components into the assembly
Applying Constraints between components
Changing the Reference set of a component
Inserting a sub-assembly into an assembly
Creating Exploded Views

Chapter 4: Creating Drawings

Starting an new Drawing file
Editing the Drawing Sheet
Generating the Base View
Creating the Section View
Creating the Detailed View
Specifying Dimension Settings
Generating Dimensions

Adding Additional Dimensions
Adding Another Sheet to the Drawing
Generating the views using the View Creation Wizard
Generating an Exploded View of an assembly
Adding Part list
Adding Balloons

Chapter 5: Additional Modeling Tools

Creating an Helix
Creating a Datum Plane
Creating a Sweep Feature
Creating a Groove Feature
Creating a Swept feature along guide curves
Creating an Emboss Feature
Shelling the Model
Creating Threads
Creating Slots
Creating a Linear Pattern
Creating a Circular Pattern
Creating a Tube Feature
Creating Instance Geometry
Boolean Operations
Creating Chamfers

Chapter 6: Sheet Metal Modeling

Starting a New Sheet Metal File
Setting Parameters of the Sheet Metal Part
Creating the Tab Feature
Creating the Flange Feature
Creating the Contour Flange
Creating the Closed Corner
Creating the Louver
Creating the Pattern Along the curve
Creating the Bead Feature
Creating the Drawn Cutout
Creating Gussets
Creating the Mirror Feature
Creating the Flat Pattern

Introduction

NX as a topic of learning is vast, and having a wide scope. It is one of the world's most advanced and highly integrated CAD/CAM/CAE product. NX delivers a great value to enterprises of all sizes by covering the entire range of product development. It speeds up the design process by simplifying complex product designs.

This tutorial book provides a step-by-step approach for users to learn NX8.5. It is aimed for those with no previous experience with NX. However, users of previous versions of NX may also find this book useful for them to learn the new enhancements. The user will be guided from starting a NX8.5 session to creating parts, assemblies, and drawings. Each chapter has components explained with the help of various dialog boxes and screen images.

Scope of this Book

This book is written for students and engineers who are interested to learn NX8.5 for designing mechanical components and assemblies, and then create drawings.

This book provides a step-by-step approach for learning NX8.5. The topics include Getting Started with NX8.5, Basic Part Modeling, Creating Assemblies, Creating Drawings, Additional Modeling Tools, and Sheet Metal Modeling.

Chapter 1 gives an introduction to NX8.5. The user interface, terminology, mouse functions, and shortcut keys are discussed in this chapter.

Chapter 2 takes you through the creation of your first NX model. You create simple parts.

Chapter 3 teaches you to create assemblies. It explains the Top-down and Bottom-up approaches for designing an assembly. You create an assembly using the Bottom-up approach.

Chapter 4 teaches you to create drawings of the models created in the earlier chapters. You will also learn to create exploded views, and part list of an assembly.

Chapter 5: In this chapter, you will learn additional modeling tools to create complex models.

Chapter 6 introduces you to NX Sheet Metal design. You will create a sheet metal part using the tools available in the NX Sheet Metal environment.

1
Getting Started

This tutorial book brings in the most commonly used features of the NX.

In this chapter, you will:

- *Understand the terminology*
- *Start a new file*
- *Understand the User Interface*
- *Understand different environments in NX*

In this chapter, you will learn some of the most commonly used features of NX. Also, you will learn about the user interface.

- In NX, you create 3D parts and use them to create 2D drawings and 3D assemblies.

- **NX is Feature Based.** Features are shapes that are combined to build a part. You can modified these shapes individually.

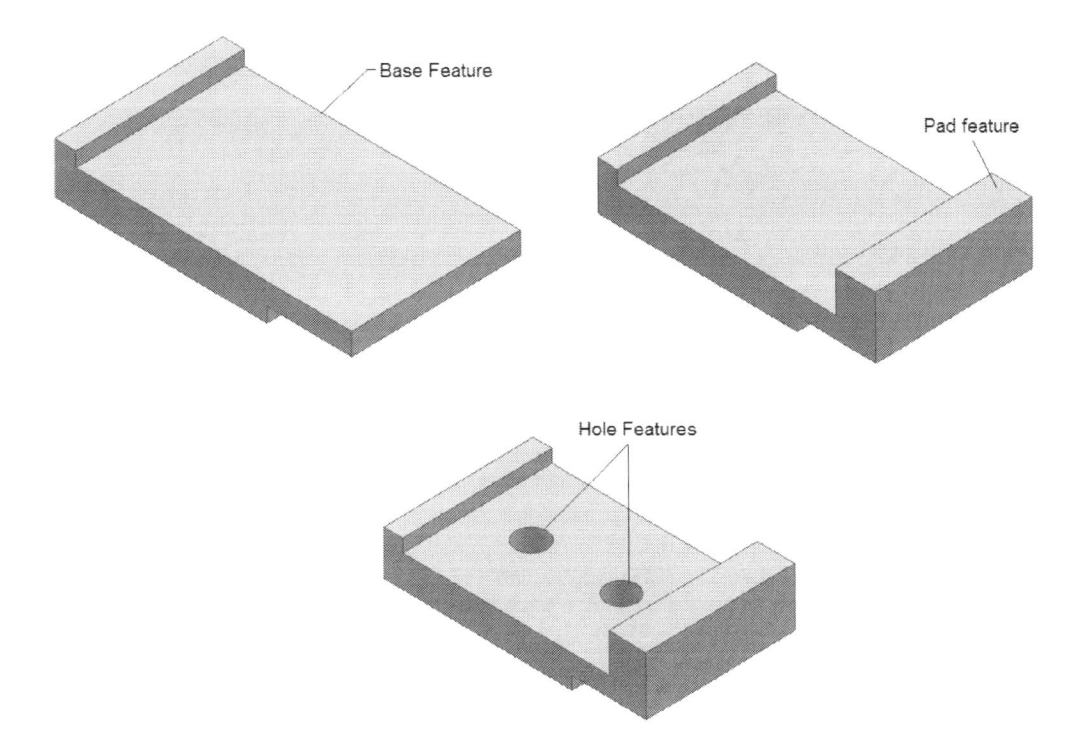

- Most of the features are sketch-based. A sketch is a 2D profile and can be extruded, revolved, or swept along a path to create features.

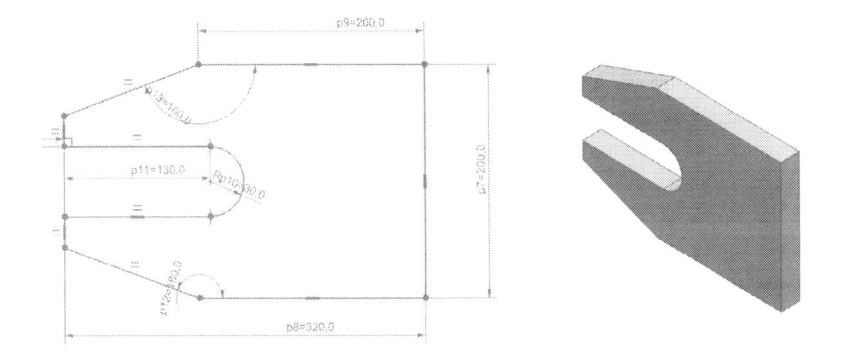

- **NX is parametric in nature.** You can specify standard parameters between the elements. Changing these parameters changes the size and shape of the part. For example, see the design of the body of a flange before and after modifying the parameters of its features

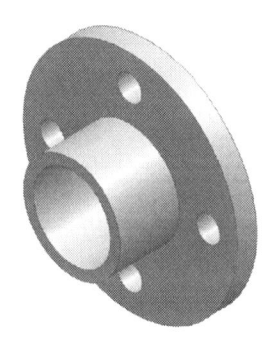

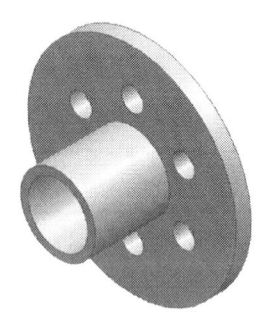

Starting NX

1. Click the **Start** button on the Windows taskbar.
2. Click **All Programs**.
3. Click **Siemens NX 8.5**.
4. Click **NX 8.5**.
5. Click the **New** button.
6. From the **New** dialog, click **Templates > Model**.
7. Click **OK** button

Notice these important features of the NX window.

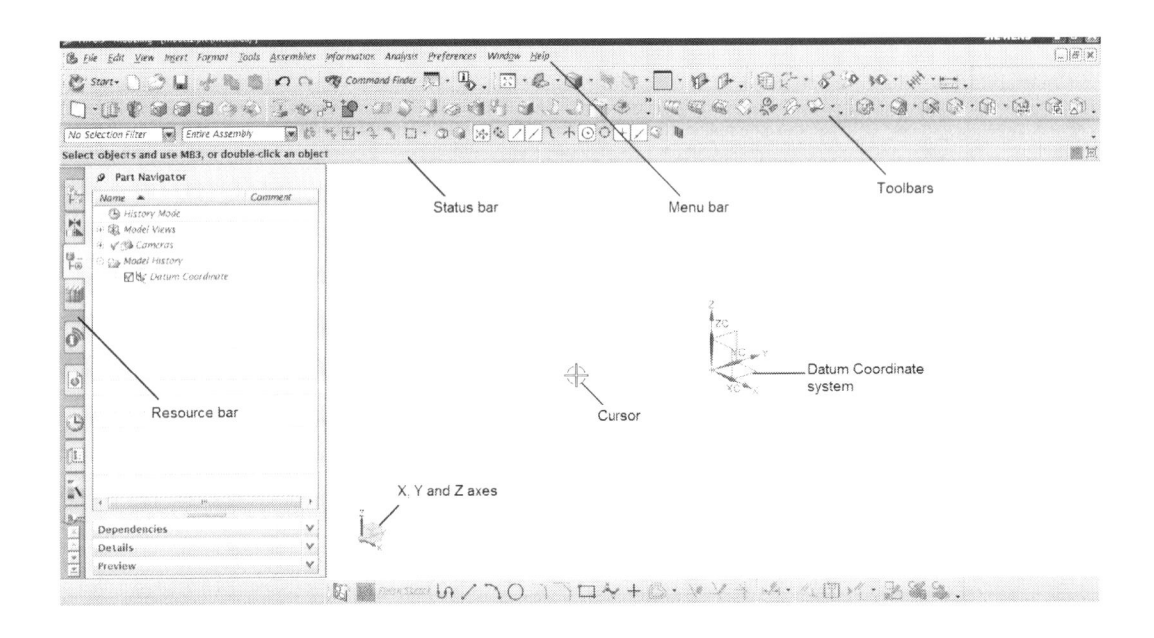

User Interface
Various components of the user interface are discussed next.

Menu bar
Menu bar is located at the top of the window. It consists of various options (menu titles). When you click on a menu title, a drop-down appears. You can select the required option from this drop-down.

Toolbars
A toolbar is a set of tools which are available in the menu bar as well. Various toolbars available in NX are discussed next.

Standard Toolbar
This toolbar contains the tools such as **New**, **Open**, **Save** and so on. You can open all the applications using the **Start** drop-down available in this toolbar.

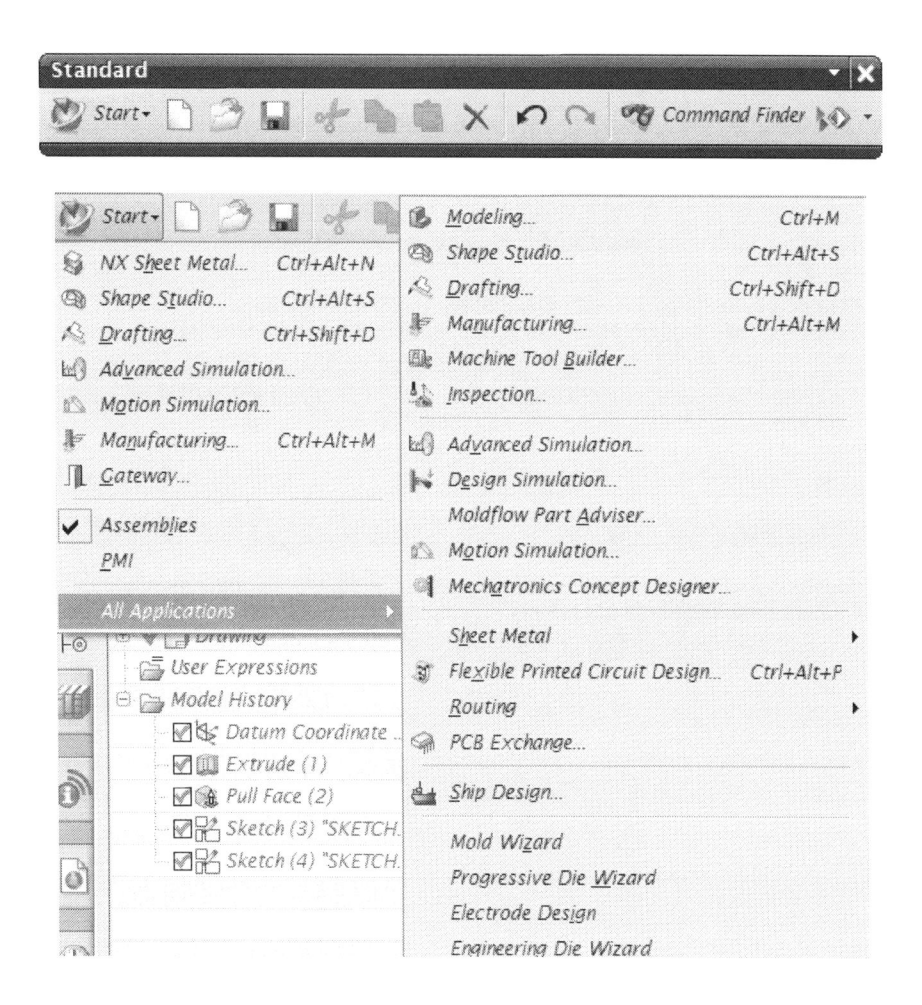

View Toolbar
This toolbar contains the tools to modify the display of the model.

Utility Toolbar
This toolbar also contains some view modification tools. It also has the tools to measure the objects.

Direct Sketch Toolbar
This toolbar contains all the sketch tools. Using this toolbar, you can directly draw sketches in the modeling environment.

Sketch Task Environment Toolbars
You can also draw a sketch in a separate environment called Sketch task environment. The toolbars in this environment contain the same tools as in the **Direct Sketch** toolbar.

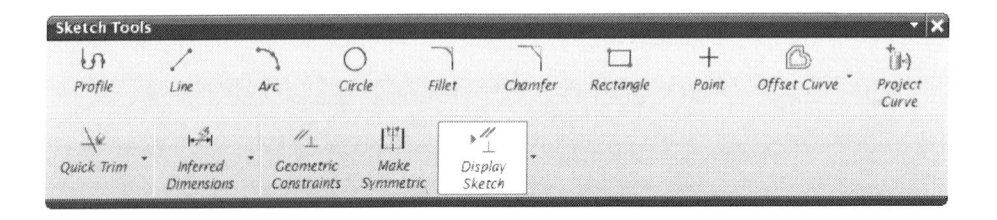

Feature Toolbar
This toolbar contains the tools to create 3D features.

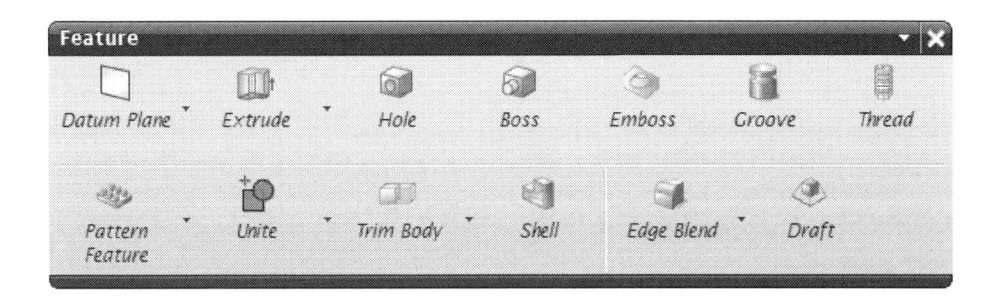

Surface Toolbar
This toolbar contains the tools to create surface features.

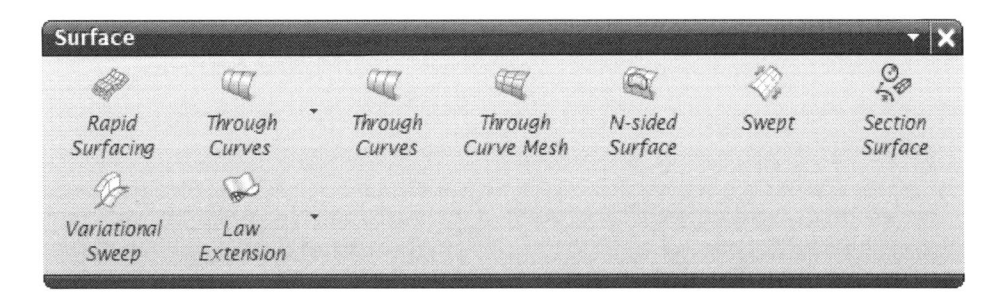

Assemblies Toolbar
This toolbar contains the tools to create an assembly.

Exploded Views Toolbar
This toolbar contains the tools to create the exploded views of an assembly.

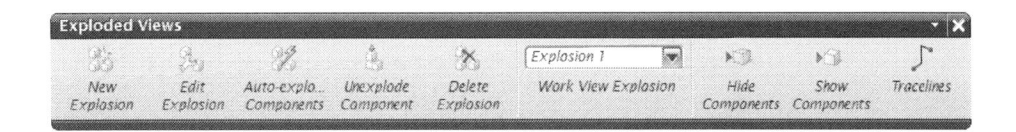

Drafting Environment Toolbars

In the Drafting Environment, you can create orthographic views of the 3D model. The toolbars in this environment contain tools to create 2D drawings.

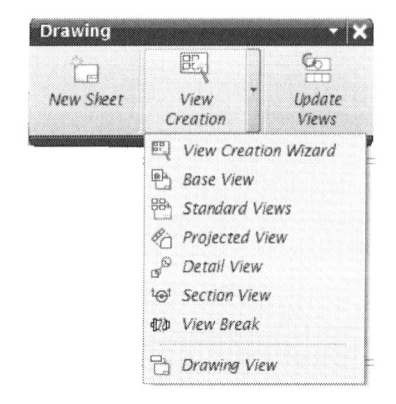

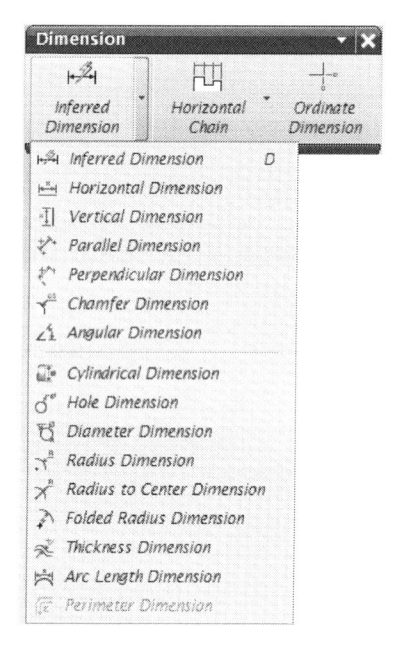

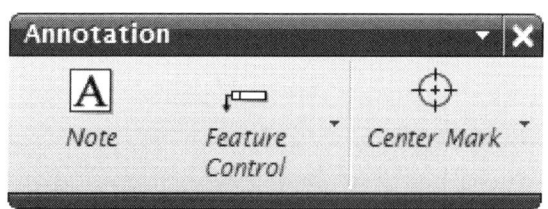

NX Sheet Metal Toolbar

The tools in this toolbar are used to create sheet metal components.

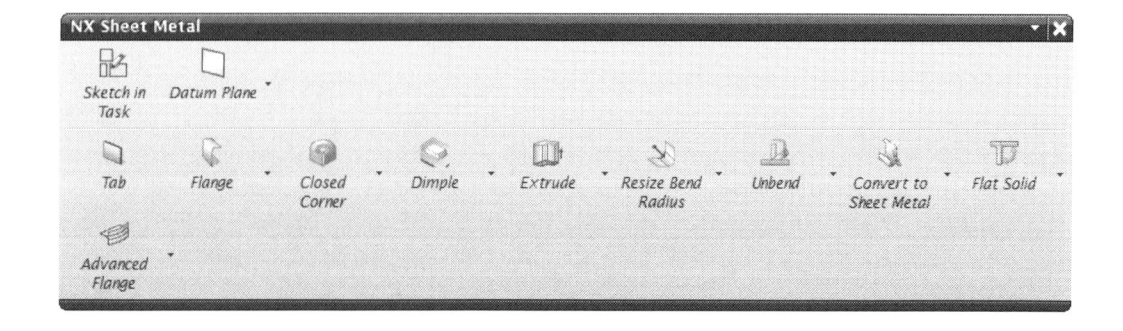

Some toolbars are not visible by default. To display a particular toolbar, right-click on anyone of the toolbar and select it from the list displayed.

- ✓ Selection Bar
- ✓ Standard
- Repeat Command
- ✓ View
- ✓ Utility
- Visualization
- True Shading
- Visualize Shape
- Analyze Shape
- Movie
- Journal
- Visual Reporting
- Check-Mate
- Application
- ✓ Assemblies
- Exploded Views
- Active Mockup
- Knowledge Fusion
- Reuse Library
- Curve
- Lines and Arcs

You can also add a toolbar by opening the **Customize** dialog box.

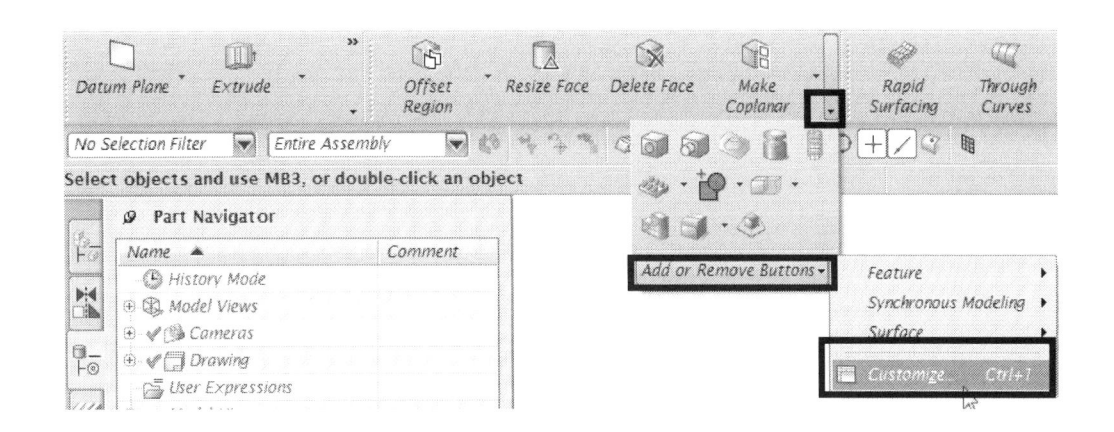

Selection bar
This is available below the toolbars. It consists of all the options to filter the objects that can be selected from the graphics window.

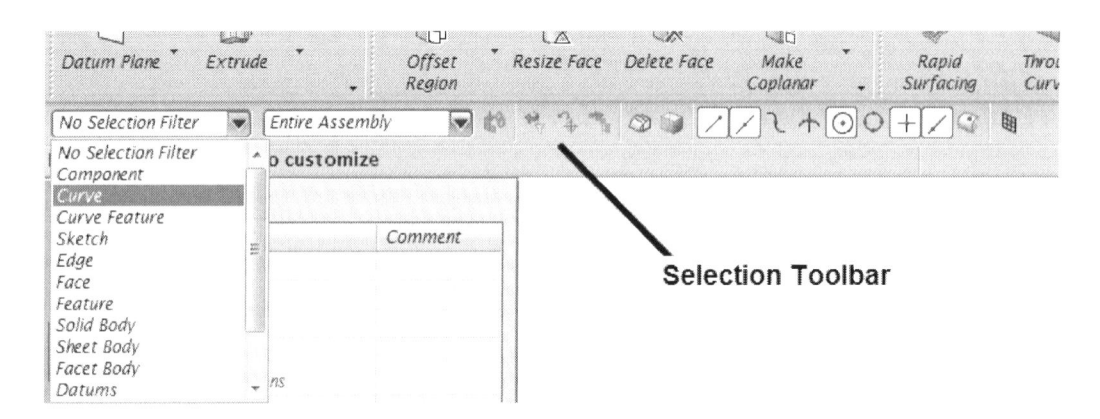

Selection Toolbar

Status bar
This is available below the Selection bar. It displays the prompts and the action taken while using the tools.

Resource Bar
This is located at the left side of the window. It contains all the navigator windows such as Assembly Navigator, Constraint Navigator, Part Navigator, and so on.

Part Navigator
Contains the list of operations carried while creating a part.

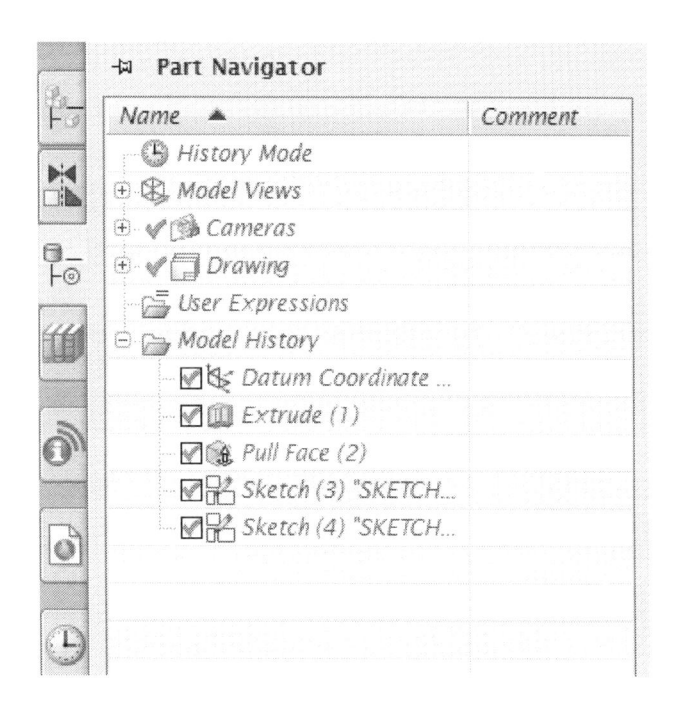

Roles Navigator
Contains the list of system default and industry specific roles. A role is a set of tools and toolbars customized for a specific application. For example, the **CAM Express** role can be used for performing manufacturing operations. This textbook uses the **Essentials with full menus** role.

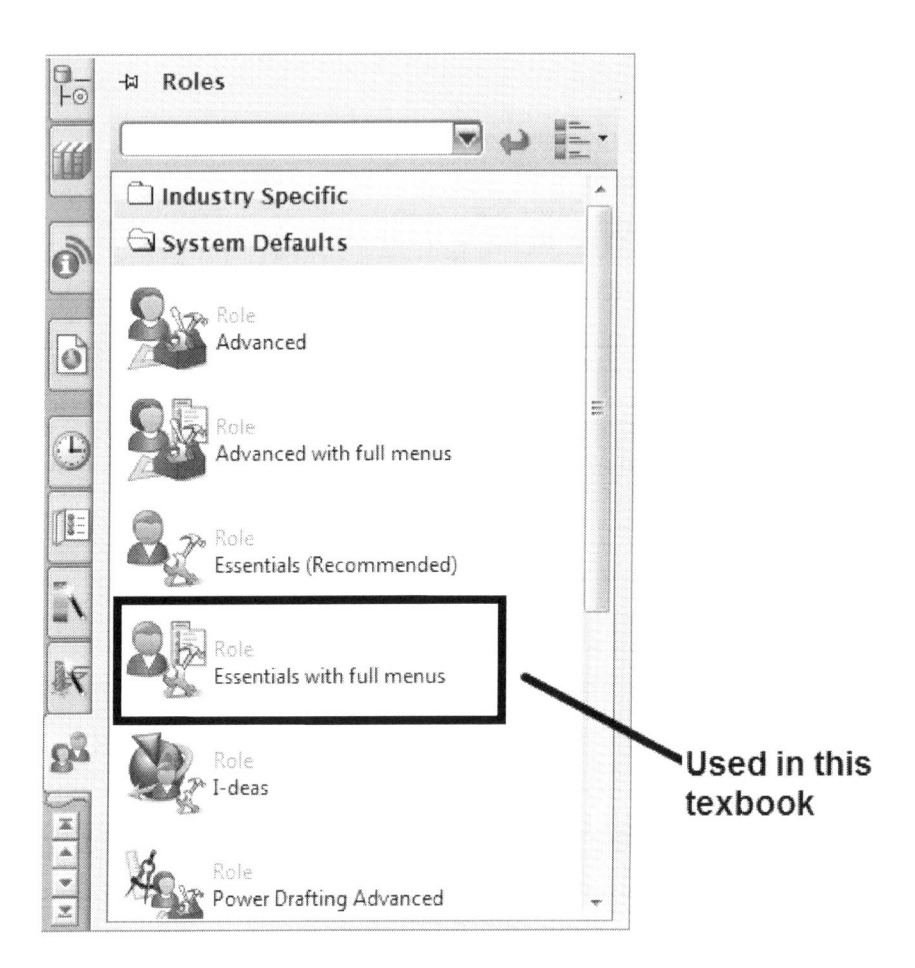

Dialog Boxes
When you execute any command in NX, the dialog box related to it appears. The dialog box consists of various options. The components of the dialog box are shown in figure.

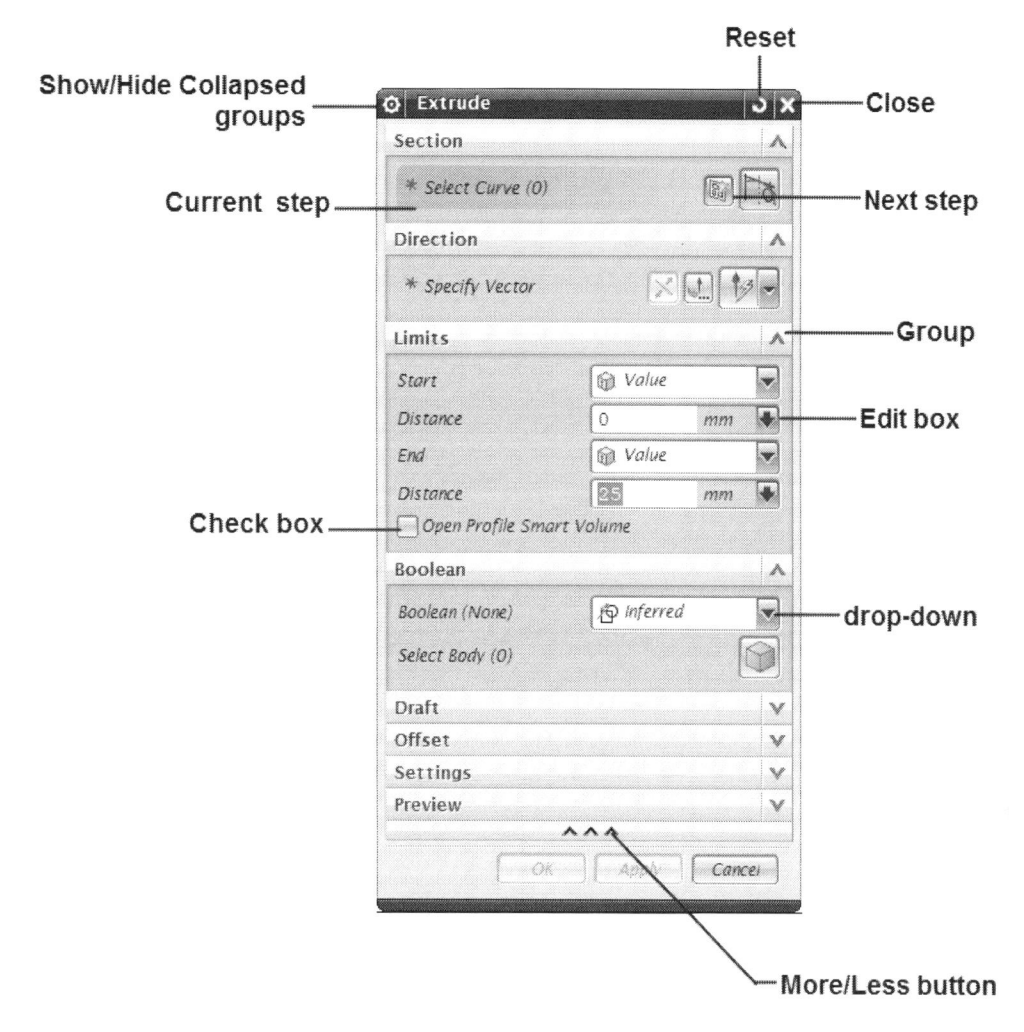

Labels on dialog box figure: Show/Hide Collapsed groups, Current step, Check box, Reset, Close, Next step, Group, Edit box, drop-down, More/Less button

This textbook uses the default options in the dialog box. If you have made any changes in the dialog box, click the **Reset** button on the dialog box; the default options will be displayed.

Mouse Functions
Various functions of the mouse buttons are discussed next.

Left Mouse button (MB1)
When you double-click the left mouse button (MB1) on an object, the dialog box related to the object appears. Using this dialog, you can edit the parameters of the objects.

Middle Mouse button (MB2)
Click this button to execute the **OK** command.

Right Mouse button (MB3)
Click this button to display the shortcut menu.

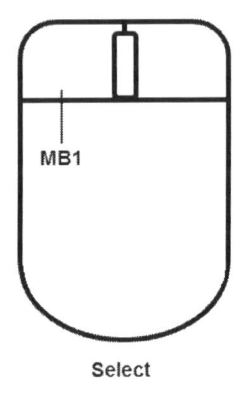

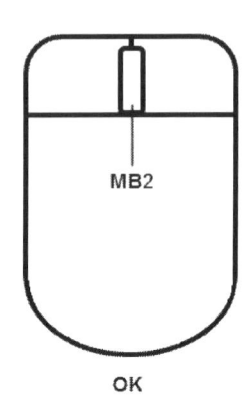

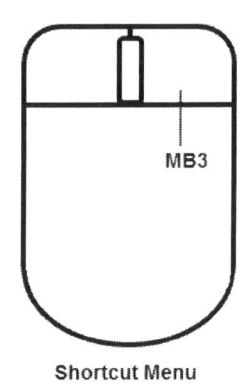

Select OK Shortcut Menu

The other functions with combination of the three mouse buttons are given next.

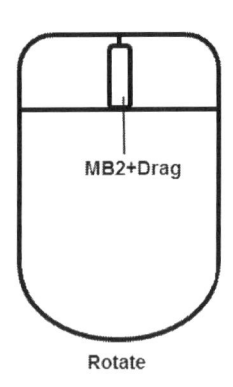

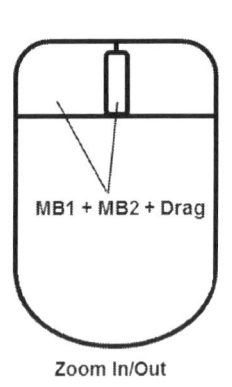

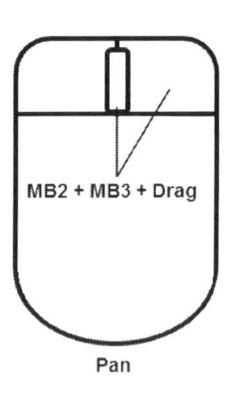

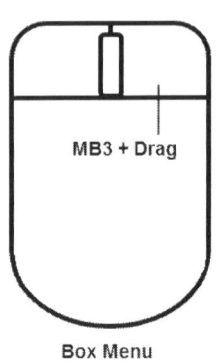

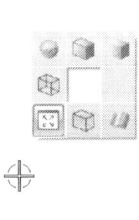

Rotate Zoom In/Out Pan

Box Menu

Color Settings

To change the background color of the window, click **Preferences > Background** on the menu bar; the **Edit Background** dialog box appears. Click **Plain** option to change the background to plain. Click on the color swatches; the **Color** dialog box appears. Change the back background color and click **OK** twice.

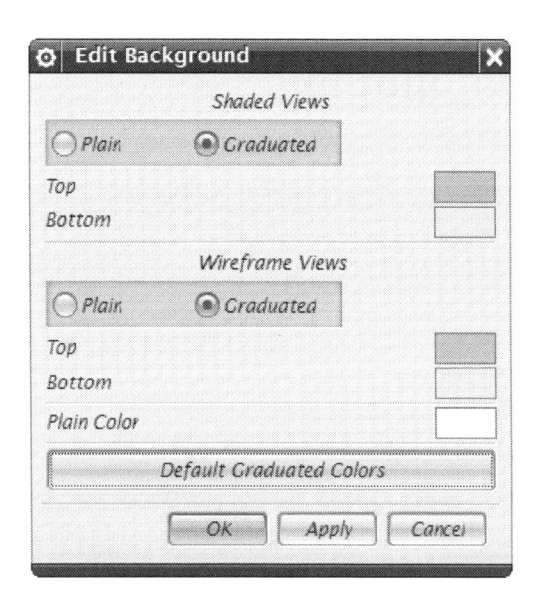

Shortcut Keys

CTRL+Z	(Undo)
CTRL+Y	(Repeat)
CTRL+S	(Save)
F5	(Refresh)
F1	(NX Help)
F6	(Zoom)
F7	(Rotate)
CTRL+M	(Starts the Modeling environment)
CTRL+SHIFT+D	(Starts the Drafting environment)
CTRL+ALT+N	(Starts the NX Sheet Metal environment)
CTRL+ALT+M	(Starts the Manufacturing environment)
X	(Extrude)
CTRL+1	(Customize)
CTRL+D	(Delete)
CTRL+N	(New File)
CTRL+O	(Open File)
CTRL+P	(Plot)

2

Modeling Basics

This chapter takes you through the creation of your first NX model. You create simple parts:

In this chapter, you will:

- *Create Sketches*
- *Create a base feature*
- *Add another feature to it*
- *Create revolved features*
- *Apply draft*

TUTORIAL 1

This tutorial takes you through the creation of your first NX model. You create the Disc of an Old ham coupling:

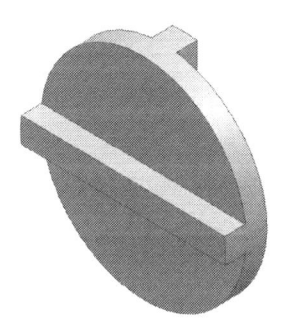

Creating a New Part File

1. To create a new part, click the **New** button on the **Standard** toolbar, or click **File > New** on the menu bar; the **New** dialog box appears.

2. The **Model** is the default selection, so click **OK**; a new model window appears.

Starting a Sketch

1. To start a new sketch, click the **Sketch** button on the **Direct Sketch** toolbar, or click **Insert > Sketch** on the menu bar; the **Create Sketch** dialog box appears.

2. Select the XZ plane.

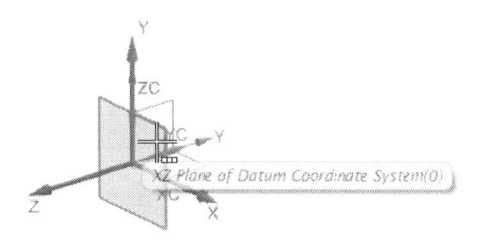

3. Click the **OK** button; the sketch starts.

The first feature is an extruded feature from a sketched circular profile. You will begin by sketching the circle.

4. Click **Circle** on the **Direct Sketch** toolbar.

5. Move the cursor to the sketch origin, and then click.

6. Drag the cursor and click to create a circle.

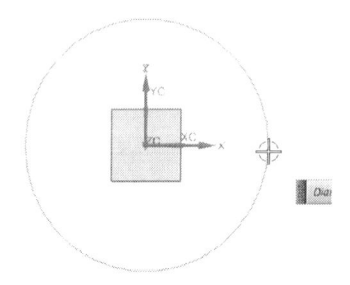

7. Press **ESC** to quit the tool.

Adding Dimensions

In this section, you will specify the size of the sketched circle by adding dimensions.

Note: You may notice that the dimensions are applied automatically. However, they do not constraint the sketch.

As you add dimensions, the sketch can attain any one of the following three states:

Fully Constrained sketch: In a fully constrained sketch, the positions of all the entities are fully described by dimensions or constraints or both. In a fully constrained sketch, all the entities are dark green color.

Under Constrained sketch: Additional dimensions or constraints or both are needed to completely specify the geometry. In this state, you can drag under constrained sketch entities to modify the sketch. An under constrained sketch entity is in maroon color.

Over Constrained sketch: In this state, an object has conflicting dimensions or relations or both. An over constrained sketch entity is red. The effected entities is in magenta color.

1. Click on the dimension displayed on the sketch; the **Dimension** edit box appears.

2. To change the dimension to 100 mm, type the value, then press **Enter**.

3. Press **Esc** to quit the **Dimension** tool.

4. To display the entire circle at full size and to center it in the graphics area, use one of the following methods:

• Click **Fit** on the **View** toolbar.
• Click **View > Operation > Fit**.
• Press the **F4** key.

You can also enter the input values while drawing a sketched entity. Enter the values in the edit boxes attached to the cursor.

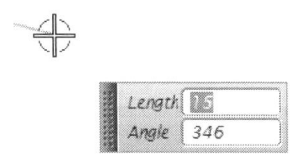

5. Click **Finish Sketch** on the **Direct Sketch** toolbar.

6. To change the view to isometric, click **Isometric** on the **View** toolbar.

You can use the buttons on the **Orient View** drop-down on the **Views** toolbar to set the view orientation of the sketch, part, or assembly.

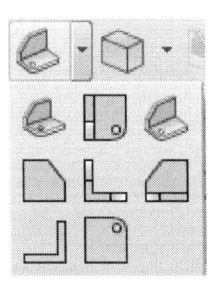

Creating the Base Feature

The first feature in any part is called a base feature. You now create this feature by extruding the sketched circle.

1. Click **Extrude** on the **Feature** toolbar, or click **Insert > Design Feature > Extrude**; the **Extrude** dialog box appears.

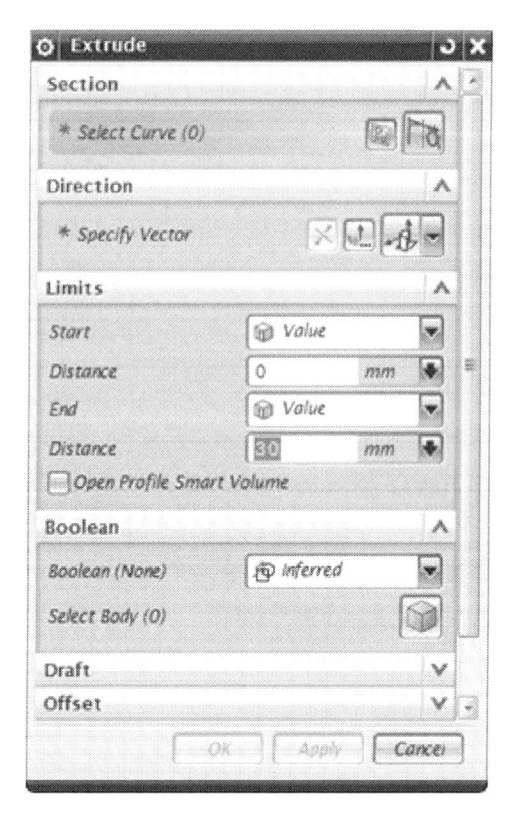

2. Enter 20 mm in the **Distance** edit box below the **End** drop-down.

3. To see how the model would look if you extruded the sketch in the opposite direction, click **Reverse Direction** button in the **Direction** group. Again click on it to extrude the sketch as shown.

4. Make sure that **Body Type** in **Settings** group is set to **Solid**.

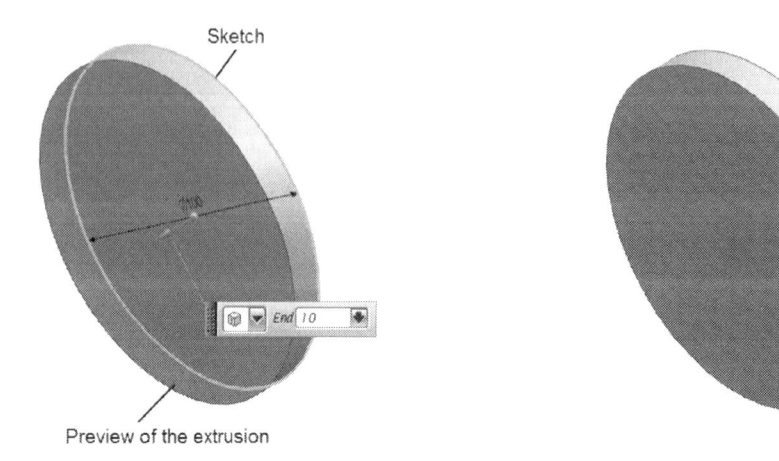

5. Click **OK** to create the extrusion.

   Notice the new feature, **Extrude**, in the **Part Navigator**.

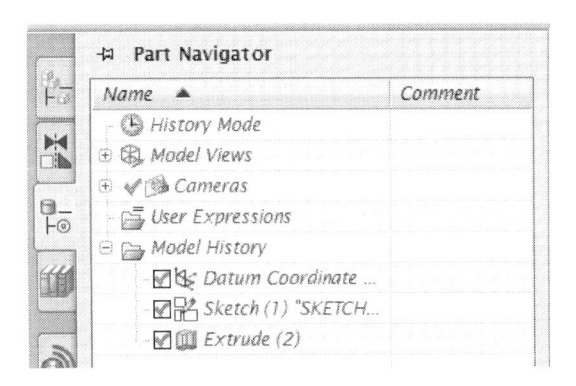

   To magnify a model in the graphics area, you can use the view operation tools available on the **View** toolbar.

Click **Fit** to display the part full size in the current window.

Click **Zoom**, then drag the pointer to create a rectangle; the area in the rectangle zooms to fill the window.

Click **Zoom In/Out**, then drag the pointer. Dragging up zooms out; dragging down zooms in.

Click a vertex, an edge, or a feature, then click **Fit to Selection**; the selected item zooms to fill the window.

To display the part in different modes, click the buttons in the **Rendering Style** drop-down on the **View** toolbar.

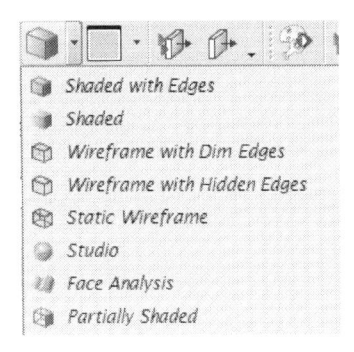

Modeling Basics

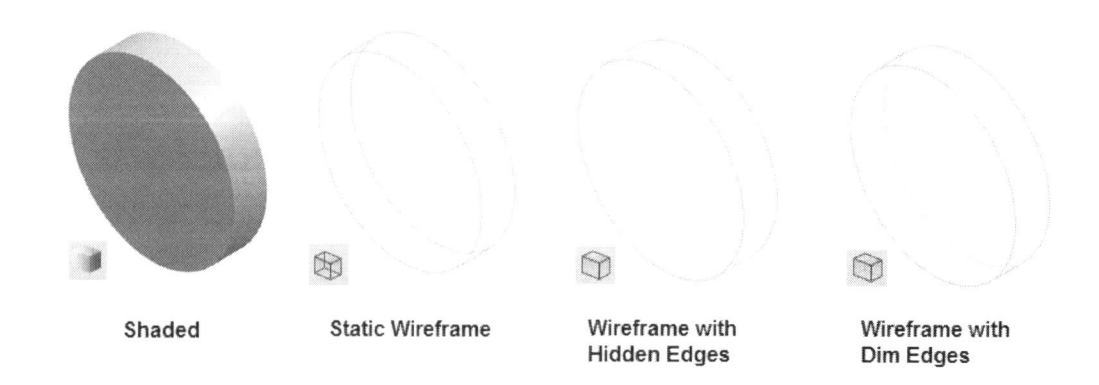

Shaded   Static Wireframe   Wireframe with Hidden Edges   Wireframe with Dim Edges

The default display mode for parts and assemblies is **Shaded with Edges**. You may change the display mode whenever you want.

Adding an Extruded Feature

To create additional features on the part, you need to draw sketches on the model faces or planes, then extrude them.

1. Click **Static Wireframe** on the **View** toolbar.

2. Click **Sketch** on the **Direct Sketch** toolbar.

3. Click on the front face of the part, and then click **OK**.

4. Click **Sketch Curve > Project Curve** from the menu bar; the **Project Curve** dialog box appears.

5. Click on the circular edge.

6. Click **OK** on the **Project Curve** dialog box; the edge is projected to the sketch plane.

7. Click **Line** on the **Direct Sketch** toolbar or click **Insert > Curve > Line** from the menu bar.

8. Click on the circle to specify the first point of the line.

9. Move the cursor towards right.

10. Click on the circle; a line is drawn.

11. Draw another line above the previous line.

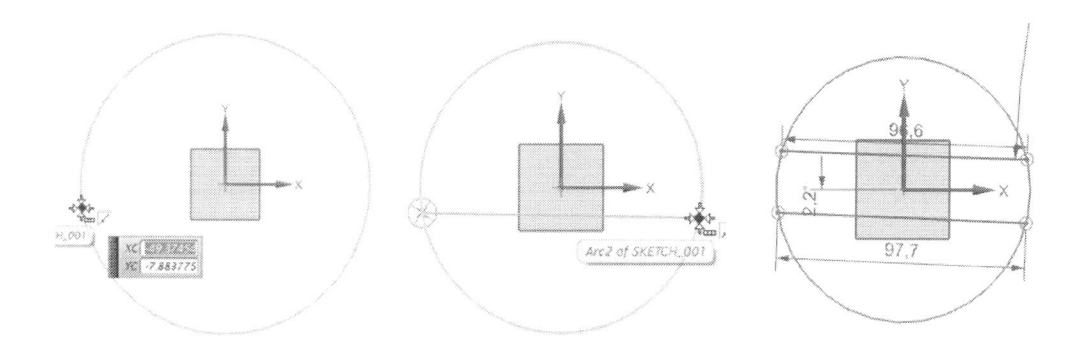

Adding Constraints and Dimensions to the Sketch

To establish the location and size of the sketch, add the necessary constraints and dimensions.

1. Click **Geometric Constraints** on the **Direct Sketch** toolbar; the **Geometric Constraints** dialog box appears.

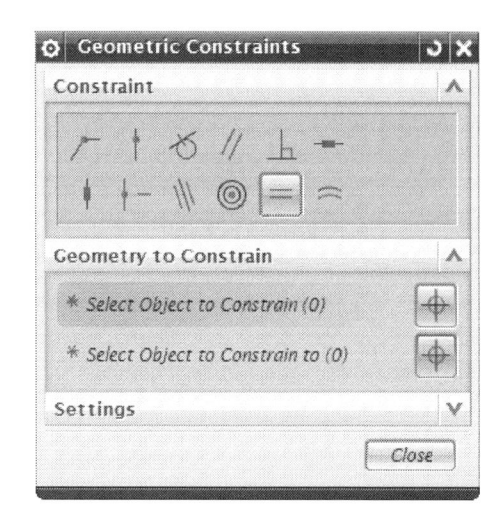

2. Click **Horizontal** in the **Constraint** group of the dialog box.

3. Click on the first line to make it horizontal.

Note
If you are applying constraints between two sketched entities, you have to first check **Automatic Selection Progression** in the **Settings** group.

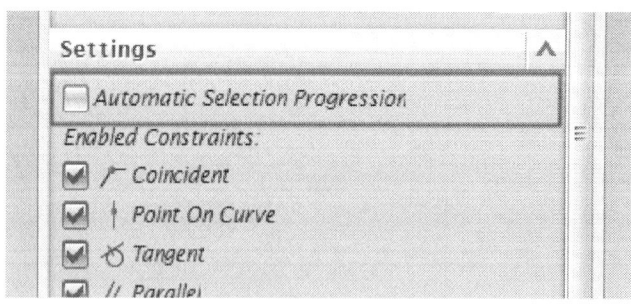

4. Click **Close** on the **Geometric Constraint** dialog box.

5. Click **Make Symmetric** on the **Direct Sketch** toolbar.

6. Select the first and second lines.

7. Select X-axis as the centerline; the two lines become symmetric about the X-axis.

8. Click **Close** on the **Make Symmetric** dialog box.

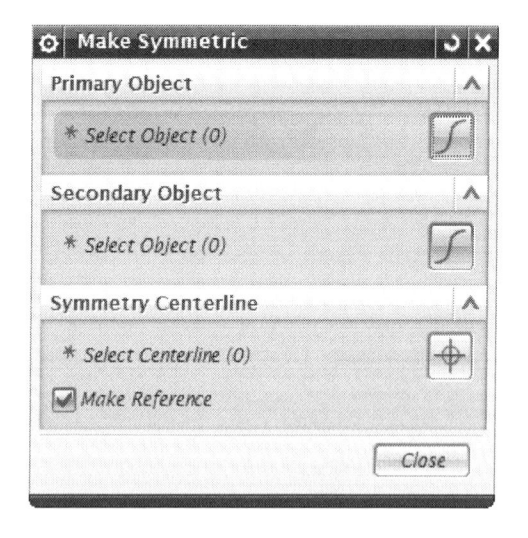

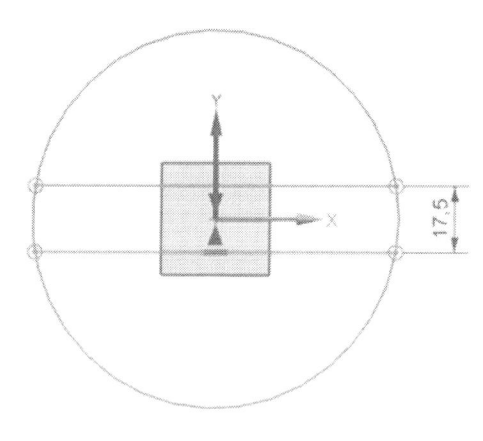

Adding Dimensions

9. Double-click on the dimension displayed in the sketch.

10. Enter 12 in the edit box displayed.

Trimming Sketch Entities

1. Click **Quick Trim** on the **Direct Sketch** toolbar.

2. Trim the projected entities.

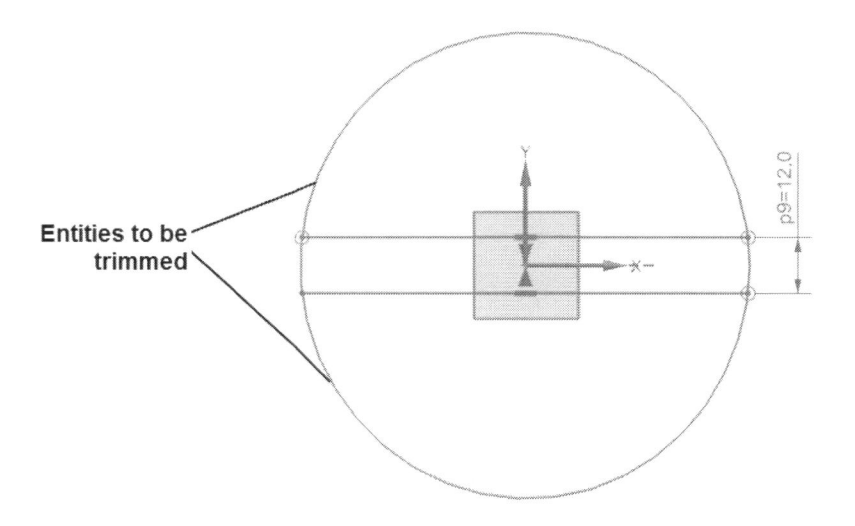

3. Click **Finish Sketch** on the **Direct Sketch** toolbar.

4. To change the view to isometric, click **Isometric** on the **View** toolbar.

Extruding the Sketch

1. Click on the sketch, and then click **Extrude** on the **Contextual** toolbar; the **Extrude** dialog box appears.

2. Enter 20 mm in the **Distance** edit box below the **End** drop-down.

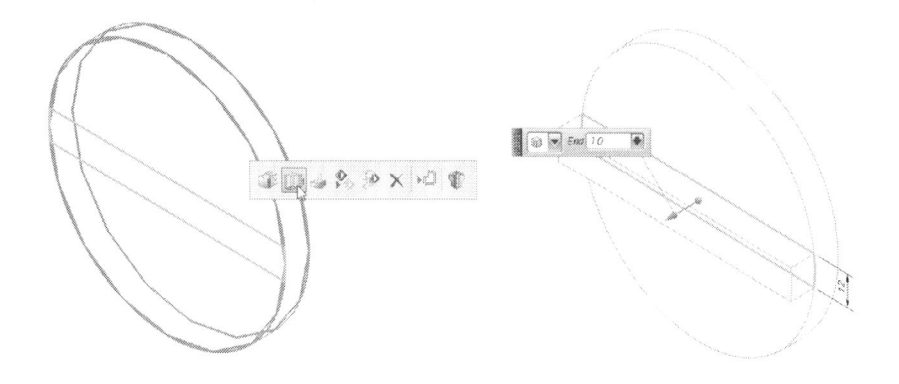

2-11   **Modeling Basics**

3. Click **OK** to create the extrusion.

4. To hide the sketch, click **Show and Hide** on the **Utility** toolbar; the **Show and Hide** dialog box appears.

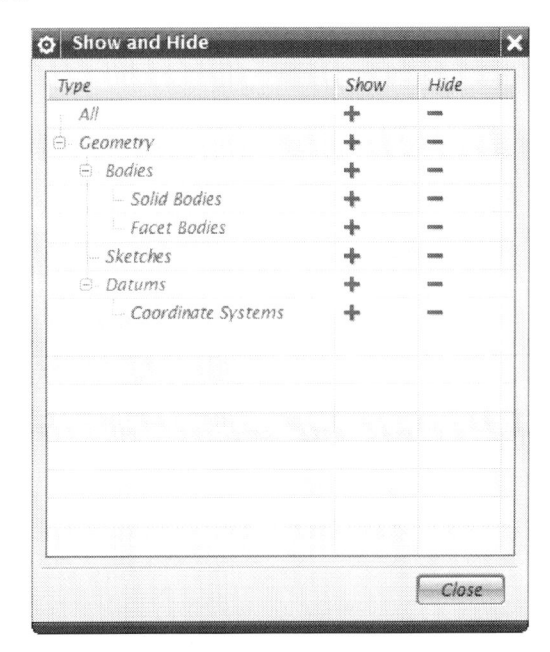

5. Click **Hide** in the **Sketch** row; the sketches are hidden.

Adding another Extruded Feature

1. Create a sketch on the back face of the base feature.

    You can use the Rotate button from the **View** toolbar to rotate the model.

2. Extrude the sketch upto 10 mm distance.

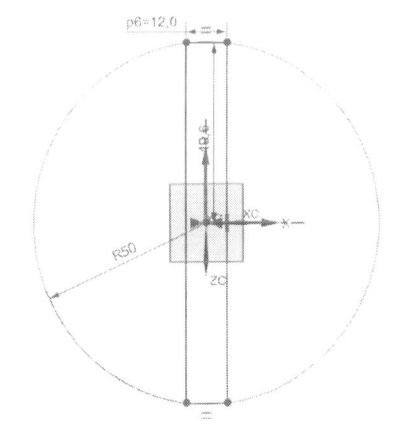

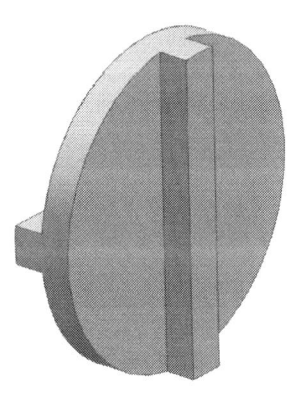

To move the part view, click **Pan** on the **View** toolbar, or click **View > Operation > Pan**, then drag the part to move it around in the graphics area.

3. Click **Shaded with Edges** on the **View** toolbar.

Saving the Part

1. Click **Save** on the **Standard** toolbar, or click **File > Save**; the **Name Parts** dialog box appears.

2. Specify **Disc** as **Name** and click **Folder** button.

3. Browse to NX 8.5/C2 folder and then click **OK** button twice.

Note:
*.prt is the file extension for all the files that are created in the Modeling, Assembly, and Drafting environments of NX.

TUTORIAL 2

In this tutorial, you create a flange by performing the following:

- Creating a revolved feature
- Creating a cut features
- Adding fillets

Creating a New Part File

1. To create a new part, click the **New** button on the **Standard** toolbar, or click **File > New** on the menu bar; the **New** dialog box appears.

2. The **Model** is the default selection, so click **OK**; a new model window appears.

Sketching a Revolve Profile

You create the base feature of the flange by revolving a profile around a centerline.

1. Click the **Sketch** button on the **Direct Sketch** toolbar.

2. Select the YZ plane.

3. Click the **OK** button; the sketch starts.

4. Click **Profile** on the **Direct Sketch** toolbar.

5. Create a sketch similar to that shown in figure.

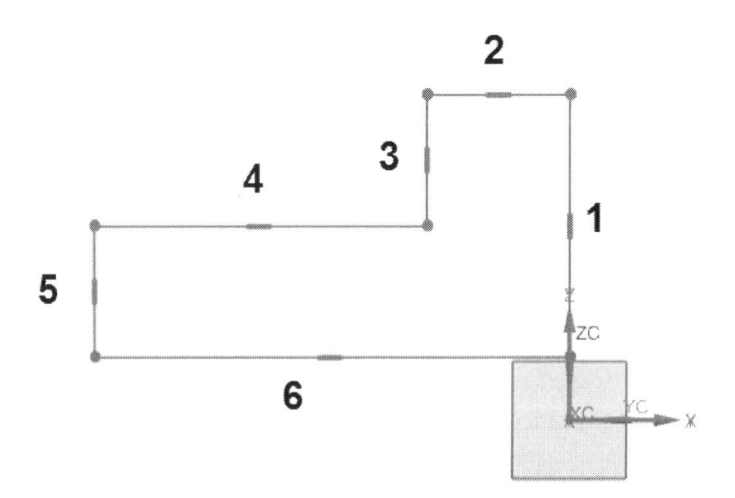

6. Click **Inferred Dimension** on the **Direct Sketch** toolbar.

7. Select the X-axis and Line 6; a dimension appears.

8. Place the dimension and enter 15 mm in the edit box.

9. Press **Enter** key.

10. Select the X-axis and Line 4; a dimension appears.

11. Set the dimension to 30 mm.

12. Select the X-axis and Line 2; a dimension appears.

13. Set the dimension to 50 mm.

14. Create a dimension between Y-axis and Line 3.

15. Set the dimension to 20 mm.

16. Create a dimension of 50 mm between Y-axis and Line 5.

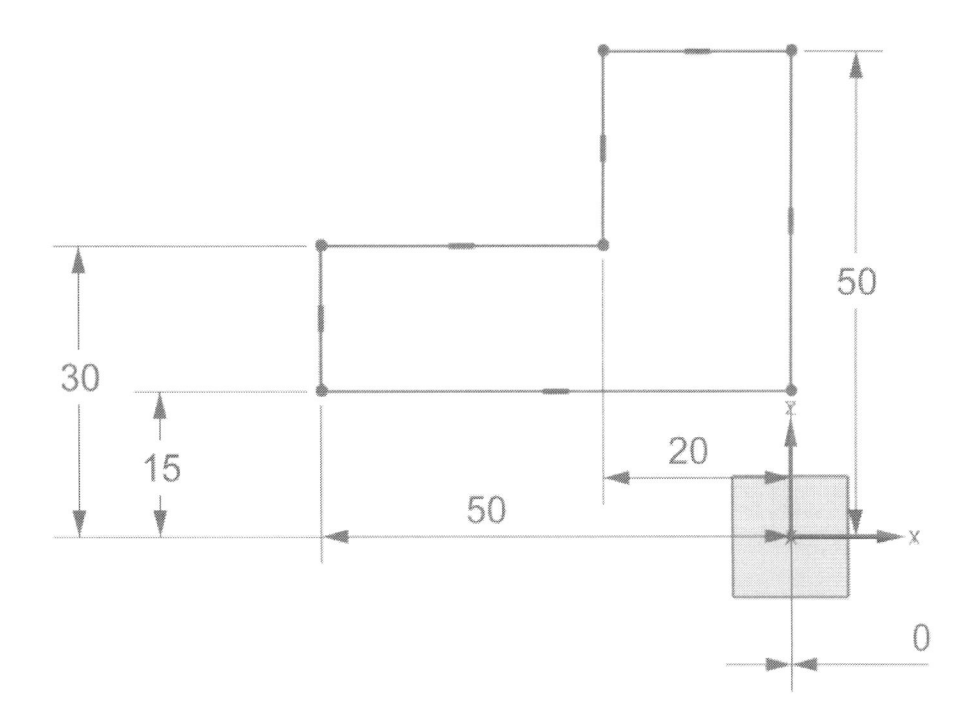

17. Click **Finish Sketch** on the **Direct Sketch** toolbar.

18. To change the view to isometric, click **Isometric** on the **View** toolbar.

Creating the Revolved Feature

1. Click the **Revolve** button on the **Feature** toolbar, or click **Insert > Design Feature > Revolve** on the menu bar; the **Revolve** dialog box appears.

2. Click on the sketch.

3. Click on **Specify Vector** in the **Axis** group; a vector triad appears.

4. Click on the Y-axis of the triad.

5. Click on the origin point of the coordinate system; the preview of the revolved feature appears.

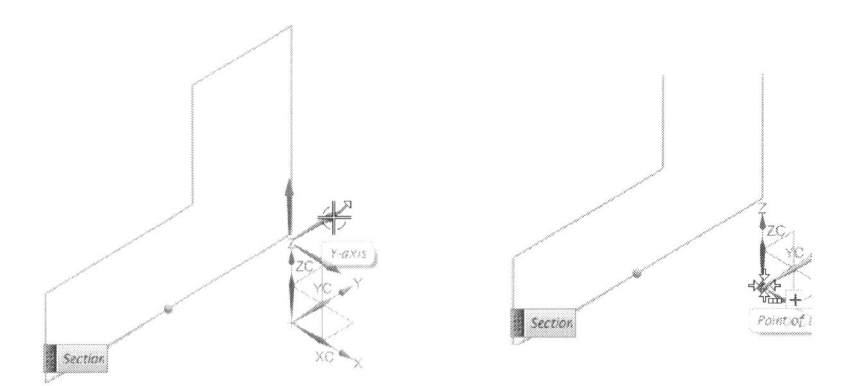

6. Set 360 degrees as **Value** below the **End** drop-down.

7. Click **OK** to create the revolved feature.

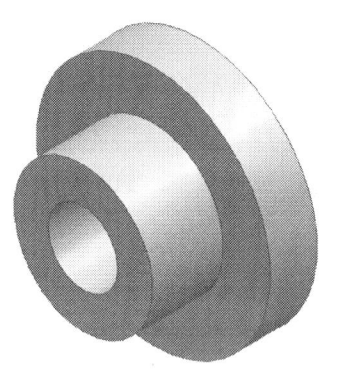

Creating the Cut feature

1. Click **Extrude** on the **Feature** toolbar, or click **Insert > Design Feature > Extrude**; the **Extrude** dialog box appears.

2. Click the back face of the part; the sketch starts.

3. Create a sketch as shown in figure.

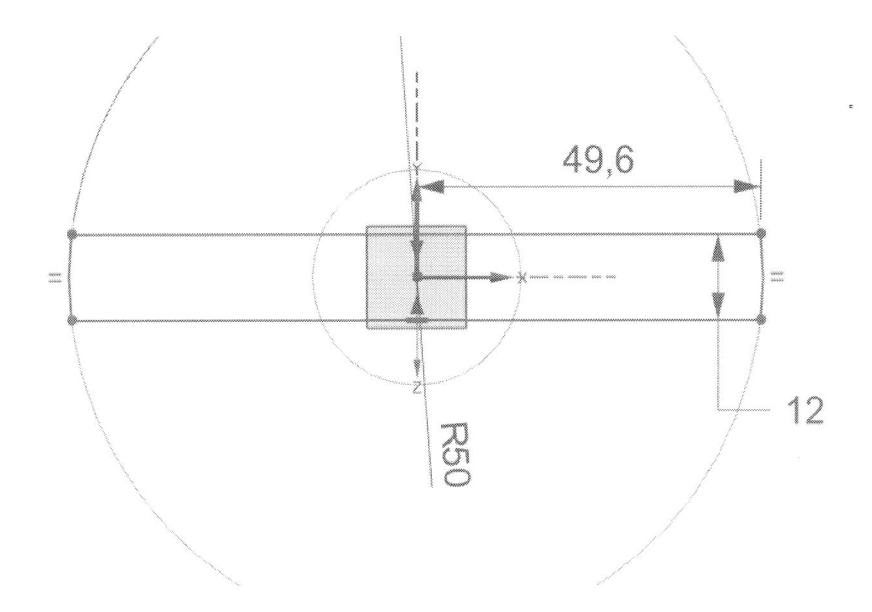

4. Click **Finish Sketch** on the **Sketch** toolbar.

5. Make sure that **Face/Plane Normal** is selected in the **Direction** group.

6. Enter 10 mm in the **Distance** edit box below the **End** drop-down.

7. Click **Reverse Direction** button in the **Direction** group.

8. Select **Subtract** in the **Boolean** group.

9. Click **OK** to create the cut feature.

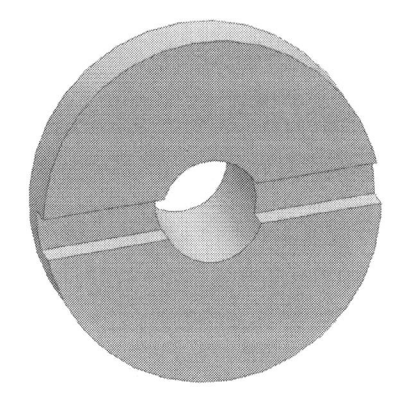

Creating another Cut feature

1. Create a sketch on the front face of the base feature.

2. Finish the sketch.

3. Click **Extrude** on the **Feature** toolbar.

4. Select **Through All** from the **End** drop-down.

5. Click **Reverse Direction** button in the **Direction** group, if required.

6. Select **Subtract** in the **Boolean** group.

7. Click **OK** to create the cut feature.

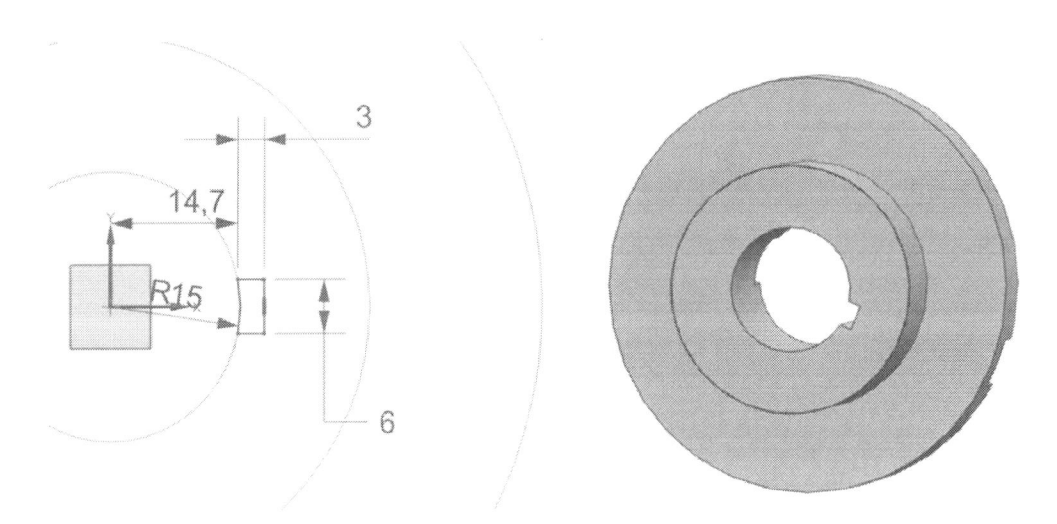

Adding Edge blend

1. Click **Edge Blend** on the **Feature** toolbar, or click **Insert > Detail Feature > Edge Blend**; the **Edge Blend** dialog box appears.

2. Click on the inner circular edge and set **Radius 1** as 5 mm

3. Click **OK** to add the blend.

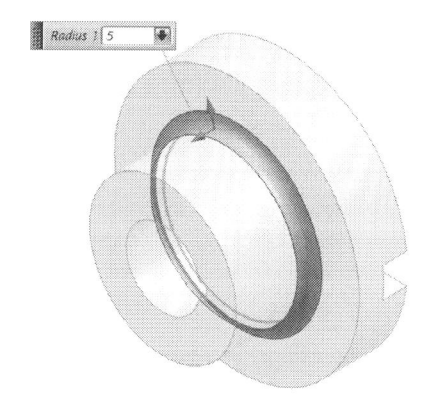

Saving the Part

1. Click **Save** on the **Standard** toolbar, or click **File > Save**; the **Name Parts** dialog box appears.

2. Type **Flange** and click **Folder** button.

3. Browse to NX 8.5/C2 folder and then click **OK** button twice.

4. Click **File > Close > All Parts**.

TUTORIAL 3
In this tutorial, you create the Shaft by performing the following:

- Creating a revolved feature
- Creating a cut feature

Creating a New Part File

1. To create a new part, click the **New** button on the **Standard** toolbar, or click **File > New** on the menu bar; the **New** dialog box appears.

2. The **Model** is the default selection, so click **OK**; a new model window appears.

Creating the Revolved Feature

1. Click the **Revolve** button on the **Feature** toolbar.

2. Click on the YZ plane to select it, and then click **OK**; the sketch starts.

3. Create a sketch as shown in figure.

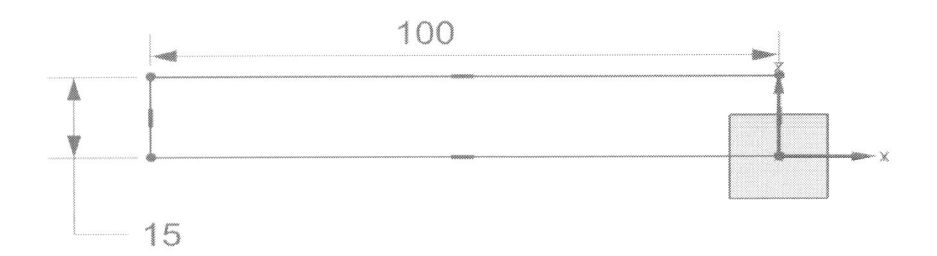

4. Click **Finish Sketch** on the **Sketch** toolbar.

5. Click on the Y-axis of the triad.

6. Click on the origin point of the coordinate system; the preview appears.

7. Click **OK** to create the revolved feature

Creating Cut feature

1. Create a sketch on the front face of the base feature.

2. Finish the sketch.

3. Click **Extrude** on the **Feature** toolbar.

4. Set 55 mm as **Distance** below the **End** drop-down.

5. Click **Reverse Direction** button in the **Direction** group, if required.

6. Select **Subtract** in the **Boolean** group.

7. Click **OK** to create the cut feature.

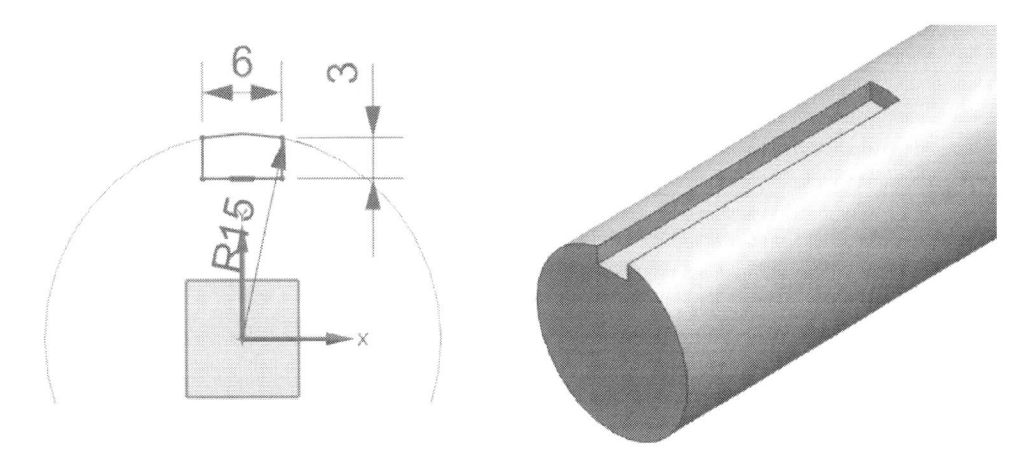

Saving the Part

1. Click **Save** on the **Standard** toolbar, or click **File > Save**; the **Name Parts** dialog box appears.

2. Type **Shaft** and click **Folder** button.

3. Browse to NX 8.5/C2 folder and then click **OK** button twice.

4. Click **File > Close > All Parts**.

TUTORIAL 4

In this tutorial, you create a Key by performing the following:

- Creating a Extruded feature.
- Applying draft.

Creating Extruded feature

1. Create a new part file.

2. Click **Extrude** on the **Feature** toolbar.

3. Select the XZ plane.

4. Create the sketch as shown in figure.

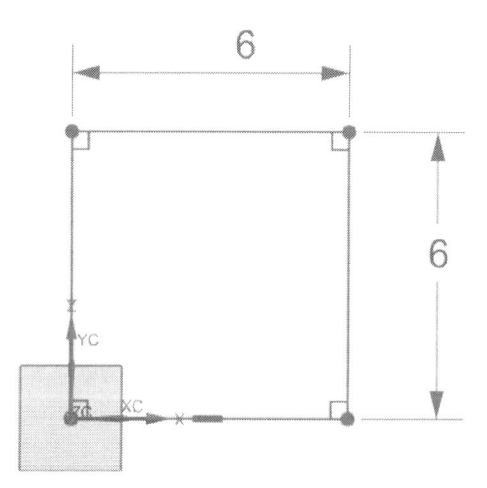

5. Finish the sketch.

6. Enter 50 mm in the **Distance** edit box below the **End** drop-down.

7. Click **OK** to create the extrusion.

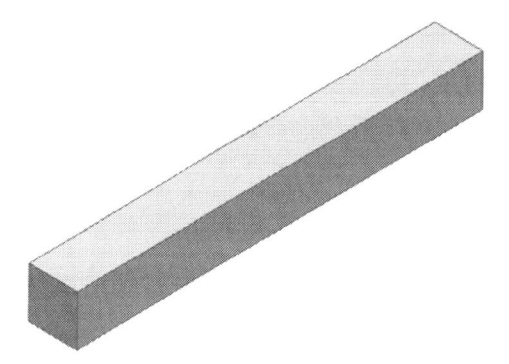

Applying Draft

1. Click **Draft** on the **Feature** toolbar, or click **Insert > Detail Feature > Draft**; the **Draft** dialog box appears.

2. Select **From Plane or Surface** from the **Type** drop-down.

3. Click on Y-axis to specify vector.

4. Select front face as the stationary face.

5. Click **Select Face** in the **Faces to Draft** group.

6. Select the top face.

7. Set 1 as the **Angle 1** in the **Faces to Draft** group.

8. Click **OK** to create the draft.

Saving the Part

1. Click **Save** on the **Standard** toolbar, or click **File > Save**; the **Name Parts** dialog box appears.

2. Type **Key** and click **Folder** button.

3. Browse to NX 8.5/C2 folder and then click **OK** button twice.

4. Click **File > Close > All Parts**.

3
Creating Assembly

In this chapter, you will:

- Add Components to an assembly
- Apply constraints between components
- Create exploded view of the assembly

TUTORIAL 1

This tutorial takes you through the creation of your first assembly. You create the Oldham coupling assembly:

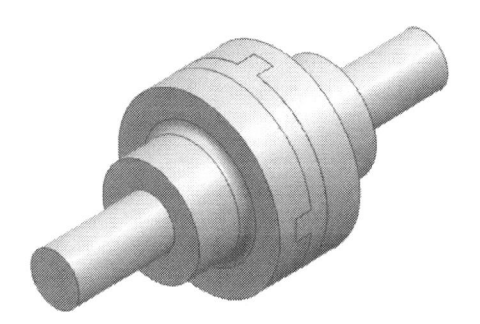

Copying the Part files into a new folder

1. Create a folder named **Oldham_Coupling** at the location NX8.5/C3.

2. Copy all the part files created in the previous chapter to this folder.

Creating a New Assemly File

1. To create a new assembly, click the **New** button on the **Standard** toolbar, or click **File > New** on the menu bar; the **New** dialog box appears.

2. Click **Assembly** in the **Template** group.

3. Click **OK**; a new assembly window appears. Also, the **Add Component** dialog box appears.

Inserting the Base Component

1. To insert the base component, click **Open** button in the **Part** group of the **Add Component** dialog box.

2. Browse to the location NX8.5/C3/Oldham_Coupling and double-click on **Flange.prt**.

3. Select **Absolute Origin** from the **Positioning** drop-down in the **Placement** group.

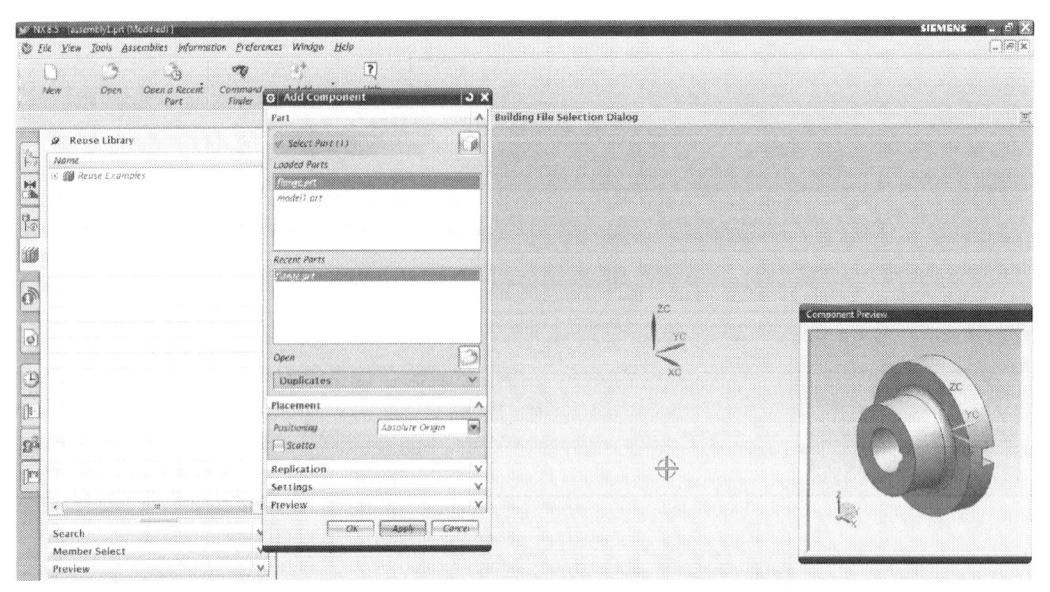

Creating Assembly

4. Select **Entire Part** from the **Reference Set** drop-down in the **Settings** group.

5. Click **OK** to place the Flange at the origin.

There are two ways of creating any assembly model.

- Top-Down Approach
- Bottom-Up Approach

Top-Down Approach
The assembly file is created first and components are created in that file.

Bottom-Up Approach
The components are created first and then added to the assembly file. In this tutorial, you create the assembly using this approach.

Adding the second component

1. To insert the second component, click **Add Component** button on the **Assemblies** toolbar, or click **Assemblies > Components > Add Component** on the menu bar; the **Add Component** dialog box appears.

2. Click **Open** button in the **Part** group of the **Add Component** dialog box.

3. Browse to the location NX8.5/C3/Oldham_Coupling and double-click on **Shaft.prt**.

4. Select **By Constraints** from the **Positioning** drop-down in the **Placement** group.

5. Select **Entire Part** from the **Reference Set** drop-down in the **Settings** group.

6. Click **OK** on the **Add Component** dialog box; the **Assembly Constraints** dialog box appears.

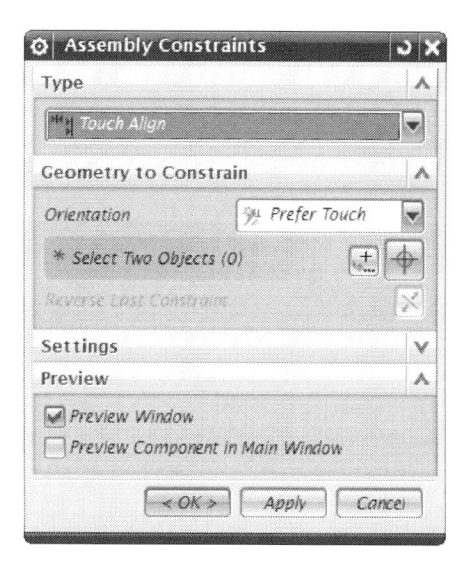

After adding the components to the assembly environment, you need apply constraints between them. By applying constraints, you establish relationships between components. Different constraints are given below.

Touch Align: Using this constraint, you can make two planar faces coplanar to each other. Note that if you set the **Orientation** as **Align**, the faces will point in the same direction. You can also align the centerlines of the cylindrical faces.

Concentric: This constraint is used to make centers of the circular edges coincident. Also, the circular edges will be on the same plane.

Distance: This constraint is used to give an offset distance between two objects.

Fix: This constraint is used to fix a component at its current position.

Parallel: This constraint is used to make two objects parallel to each other.

Perpendicular: This constraint is used to make two object perpendicular to each other.

Fit: This constraint is used to bring two cylindrical faces together. Note that they should have the same radius.

Bond: This constraint makes the selected components rigid so that they move together.

Center: This constraint is used to position the selected component at a center plane between two components.

Angle: Applies angle between two components.

7. Select **Touch Align** from the **Type** drop-down.

8. Select **Infer Center/Axis** from the **Orientation** drop-down in the **Geometry to Constraints** group.

9. Click on the cylindrical face of the Shaft.

10. Click on the inner cylindrical face of the Flange.

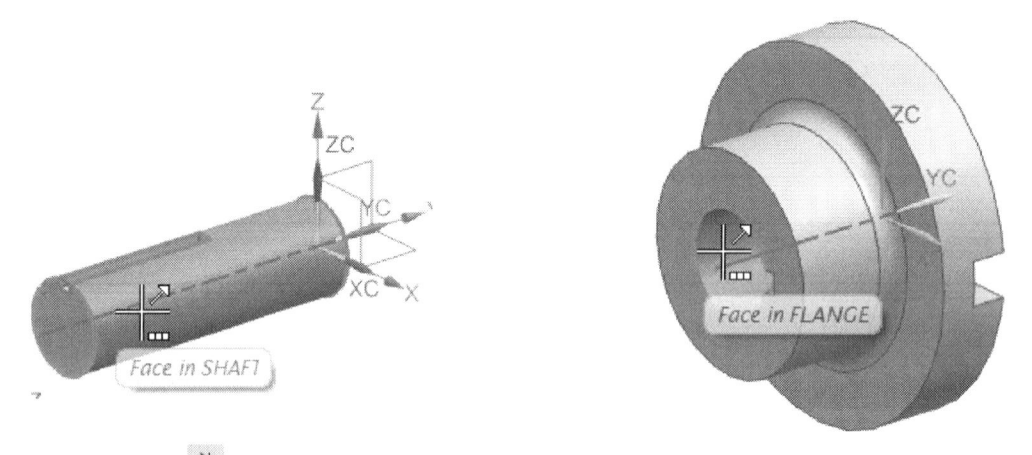

11. Select **Align** from the **Orientation** drop-down in the **Geometry to Constraints** group.

12. Click on the front face of the shaft.

13. Rotate the flange and click on the slot face as shown in figure.

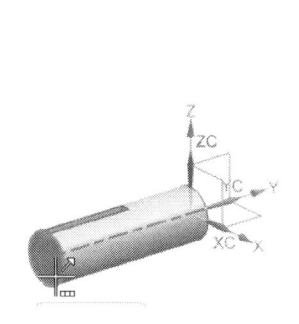

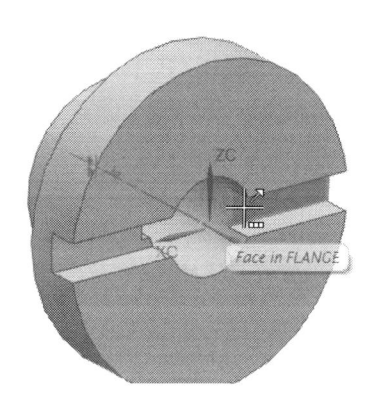

14. Click on the YZ plane of the Shaft.

15. Click on the XY plane of the Flange.

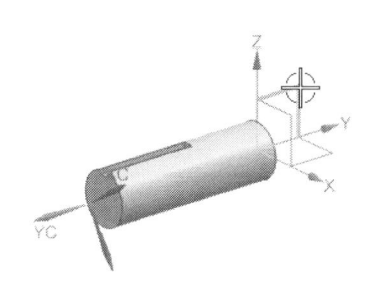

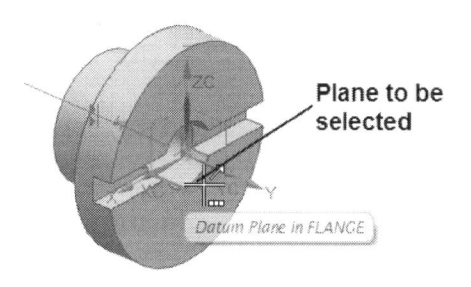

16. Click **OK** to assemble the components.

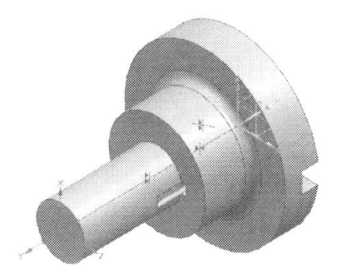

Adding the Third Component

1. Click **Add Component** button on the **Assemblies** toolbar.

2. Click **Open** button.

3. Double-click on the **Key.prt**.

4. Click OK.

5. Make sure that **Touch Align** is selected in **Type** drop-down.

6. Select **Align** from the **Orientation** drop-down in the **Geometry to Constraints** group.

7. Click on the front face of the Key and front face of the Shaft.

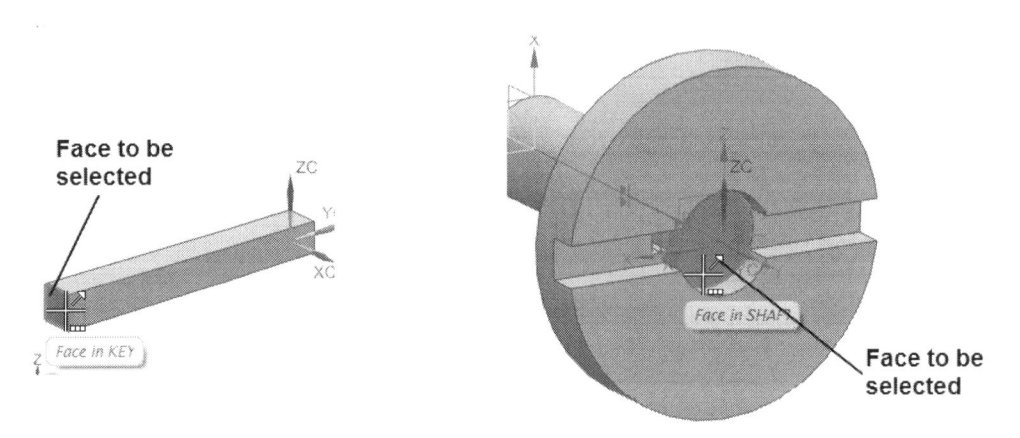

8. Click on the XY plane of the Key.

9. Click on the face on the shaft as shown in figure.

10. Select **Touch** from the **Orientation** drop-down in the **Geometry to Constraints** group.

11. Click on the side face of the Key and select the face on shaft as shown in figure.

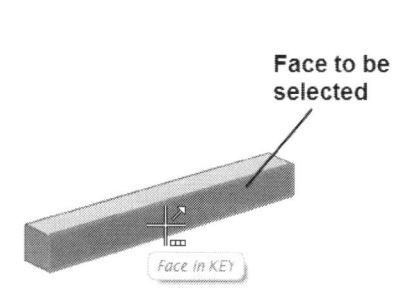

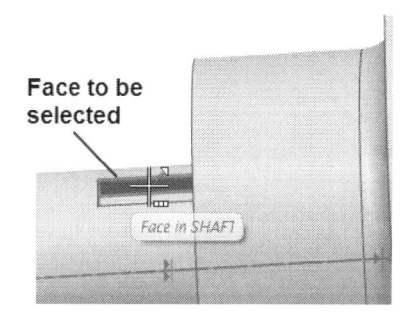

Hiding the Reference Planes

1. Click **Replace Reference Set** button on the **Assemblies** toolbar, or click **Assemblies > Replace Reference Set** on the menu bar; the **Class Selection** dialog box appears.

2. Select all the components in the assembly and click **OK**; the **Replace Reference Set** dialog box appears.

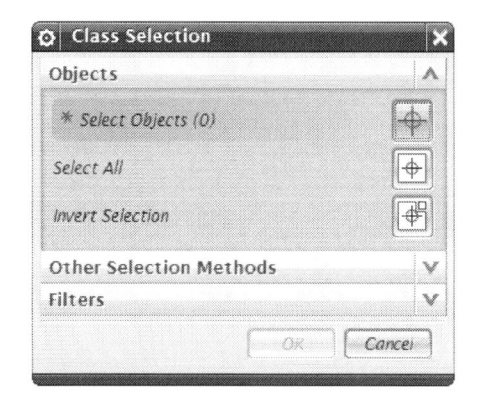

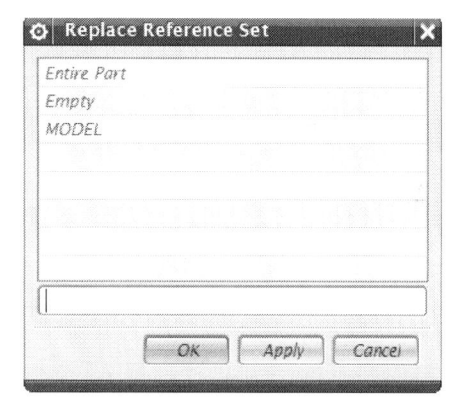

3. Click **MODEL**.

4. Click **OK** to hide the reference planes.

5. To hide the constraints, open the **Assembly Navigator**.

6. Select all the constraints and right-click.

7. Click **Hide** on the shortcut menu.

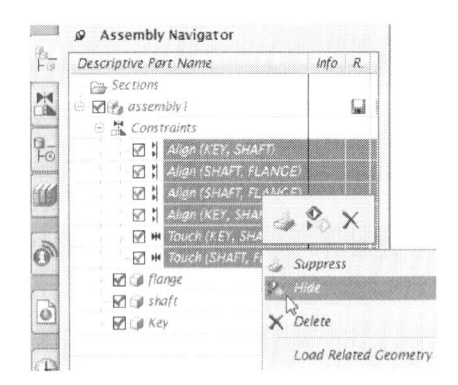

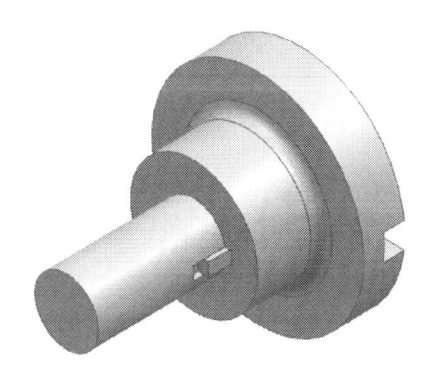

Saving the Assembly

1. Click **Save** on the **Standard** toolbar, or click **File > Save**; the **Name Parts** dialog box appears.

2. Specify **Flange_subassembly** as **Name** and click **Folder** button.

3. Browse to NX 8.5/C3/Oldham_Coupling folder and then click **OK** button twice.

4. Click **File > Close > All Parts**.

Starting the Main assembly

1. Click the **New** button on the **Standard** toolbar, or click **File > New** on the menu bar; the **New** dialog box appears.

2. Click **Assembly** in the **Template** group.

3. Specify **Main_assembly** as **Name** and click **Folder** button.

4. Browse to NX 8.5/C3/ Oldham_Coupling folder and then click **OK** button twice; the **Add Component** dialog box appears.

Adding Disc to the Assembly

1. Click **Open** button.

2. Double-click on **Disc.prt**.

3. Set **Positioning** as **Absolute Origin**.

4. Set **Reference Set** as **Model**.

5. Click **OK** to place the Flange at the origin.

Fixing the Disc to the Origin

1. Click **Assembly Constraints** button on the **Assemblies** toolbar, or click **Assemblies > Component Position > Assembly Constraints** on the menu bar; the **Assembly Constraints** dialog box appears.

2. Set **Fix** as constraint **Type**.

3. Select the Disc and click **OK**.

Placing the Sub-assembly

1. Click **Add Component** button on the **Assemblies** toolbar.

2. Click **Open** button.

3. Double-click on **Flange_subassembly.prt**.

4. Set **Positioning** as **By Constraints**.

5. Click **OK**; the **Assembly Constraints** dialog box appears.

6. Set **Type** as **Touch Align**

7. Set **Orientation** as **Touch** .

8. Click on the face on the Flange as shown in figure.

9. Click on the face on the Disc as shown in figure.

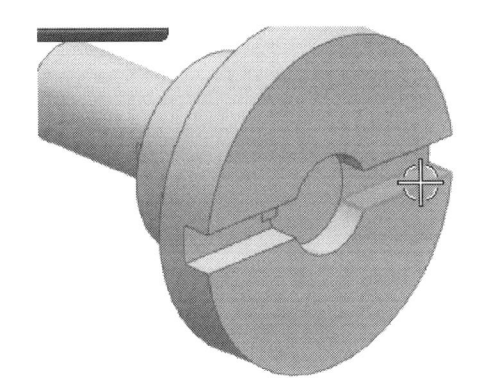

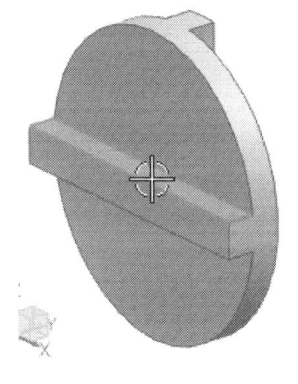

Creating Assembly

10. Set **Type** as **Concentric** ⊚ .

11. Click on the circular of the Flange.

12. Click on the circular edge of the Disc.

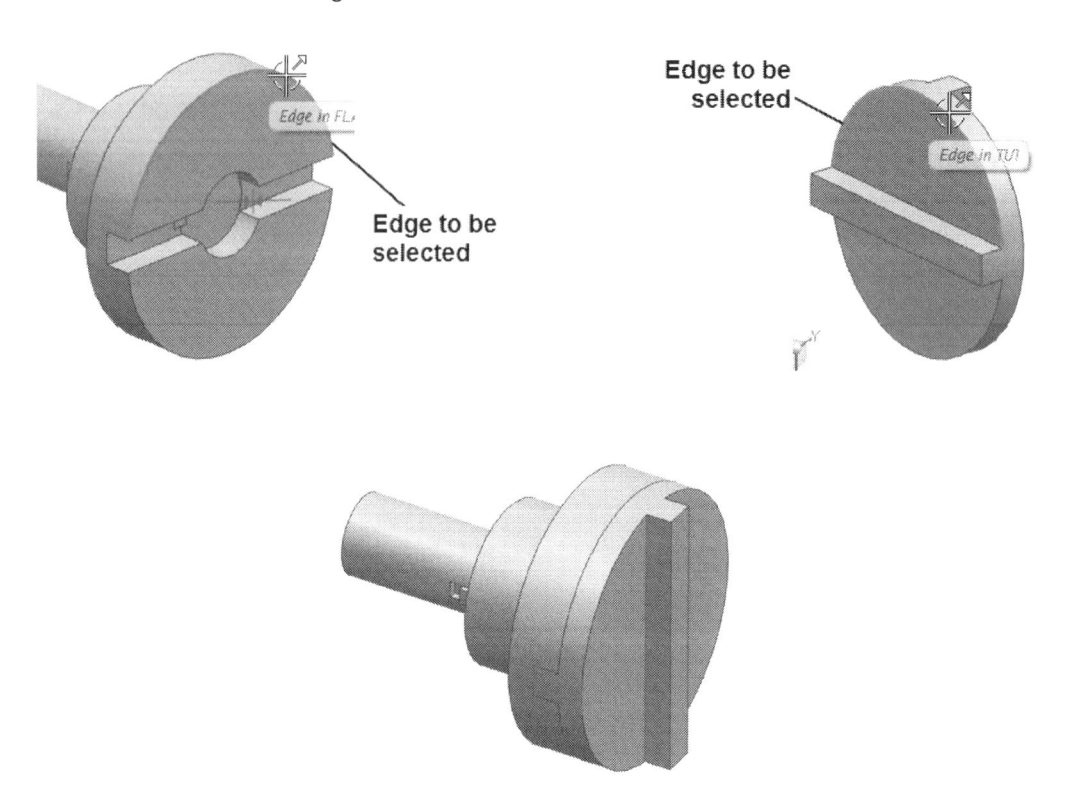

Placing second instance of the Sub-assembly

1. Insert another instance of the Flange subassembly.

2. Apply the **Touch Align** and **Concentric** constraints. Note the you have to click the **Reverse Direction** button while applying the **Concentric** constraint.

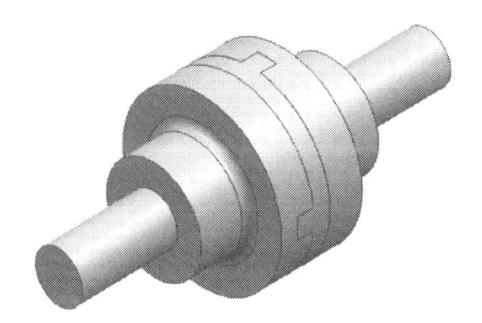

Saving the Assembly

1. Click **Save** on the **Standard** toolbar, or click **File > Save**.

TUTORIAL 2

In this tutorial, you create the exploded view of the assembly created in previous tutorial:

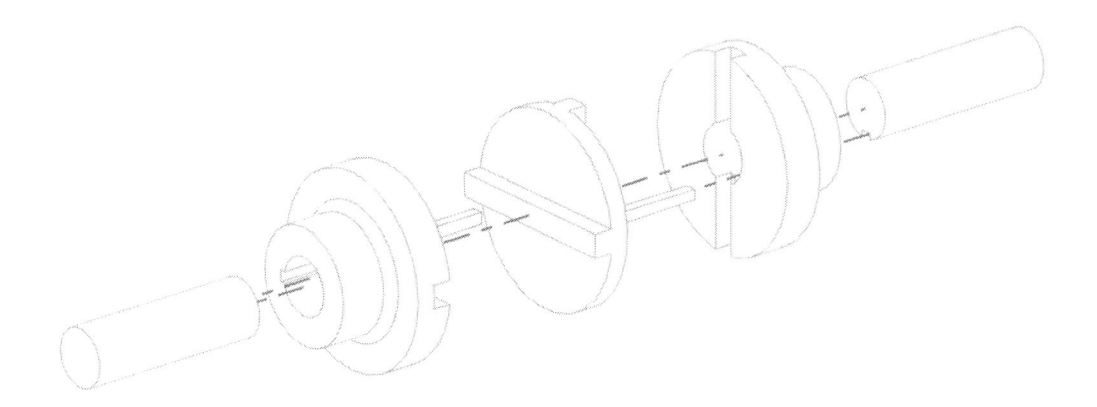

Creating the Exploded view

1. To create the exploded view, click the **Exploded Views** button on the **Assemblies** toolbar; the **Exploded Views** toolbar appears.

2. Click **New Explosion** button on the **Exploded Views** toolbar; the **New Explosion** dialog box appears.

3. Enter **Oldham_Explosion** in the **Name** edit box.

4. Click **OK**.

5. Click **Edit Explosion** button on the **Exploded Views** toolbar; the **Edit Explosion** dialog box appears.

6. Select Flange_subassembly from the **Assembly Navigator**.

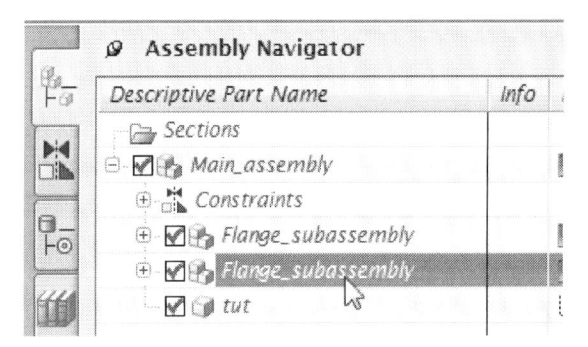

7. Click **Move Objects** on the dialog box; the dynamic triad appears on the flange subassembly.

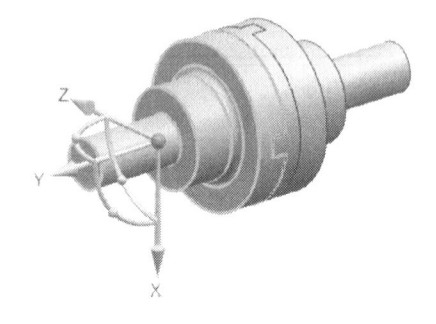

8. Click **Snap Handles to WCS** button on the **Edit Explosion** dialog box; the dynamic triad snaps to WCS.

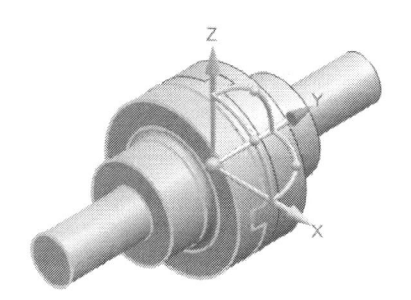

9. Click the **Y-Handle** on the dynamic triad.

10. Enter **-100** in the Distance edit box.

11. Click **OK** to explode the flange subassembly.

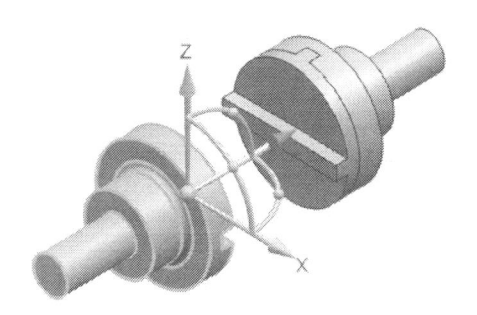

12. Click **Edit Explosion** button on the **Exploded Views** toolbar.

13. Click **Select Objects** on the **Edit Explosion** dialog box.

14. Rotate the model and select the key from the assembly.

15. Click **Move Objects** on the dialog box.

16. Click **Snap Handles to WCS** button.

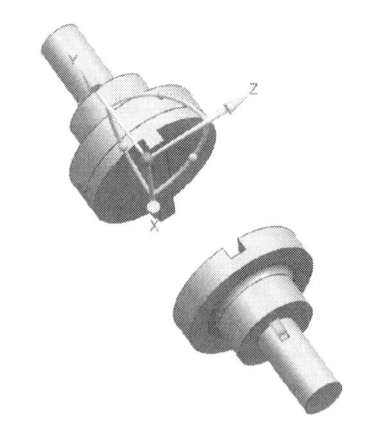

17. Click the **Y-Handle** on the dynamic triad.

18. Enter **80** in the **Distance** edit box.

19. Click **OK** to explode the key.

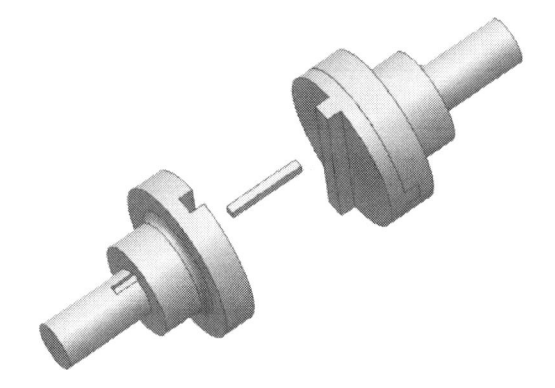

20. Invoke the **Edit Explosion** dialog box.

21. Explode the shaft in Y-direction upto to a distance of **-80 mm**.

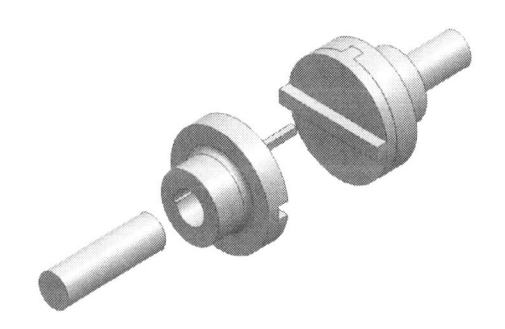

22. Similarly, explode the other flange subassembly and its parts in the opposite direction. The explosion distances are same.

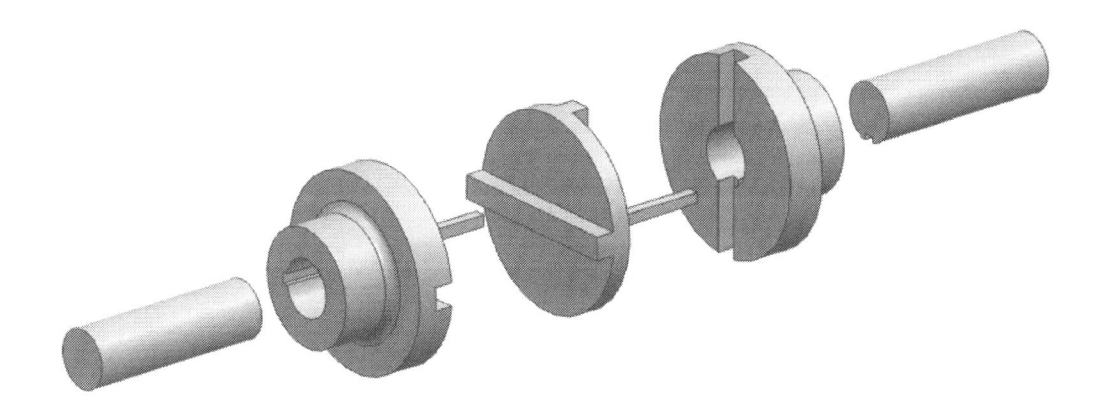

Creating Tracelines

1. To create tracelines, click the **Tracelines** button on the **Exploded Views** toolbar; the **Tracelines** dialog box appears.

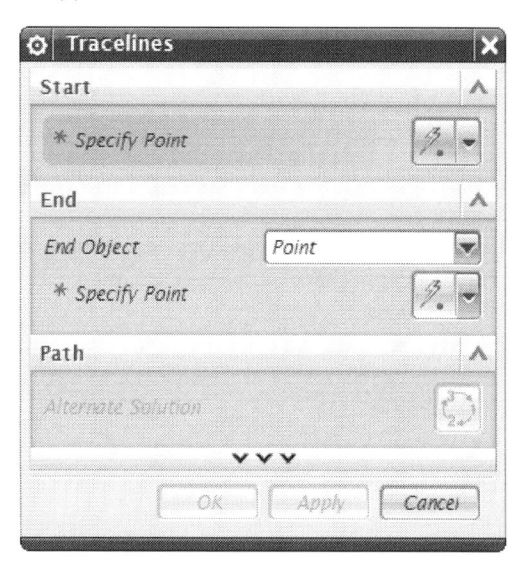

2. Select the center point of the flange.

3. Select **Component** from the **End Object** drop-down.

4. Select the shaft.

5. Click **OK** to create the traceline.

Creating Assembly

6. Click **Tracelines** button on the **Exploded Views** toolbar.

7. Select **End Point** from the **Inferred** drop-down in the **Start** group.

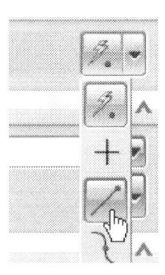

8. Select the edge on the key of the shaft.

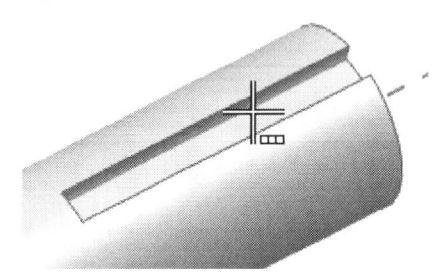

9. Double-click on the arrow displayed on the edge to reverse the direction.

10. Select **Point** from the **End Object** drop-down.

11. Select the edge on the key.

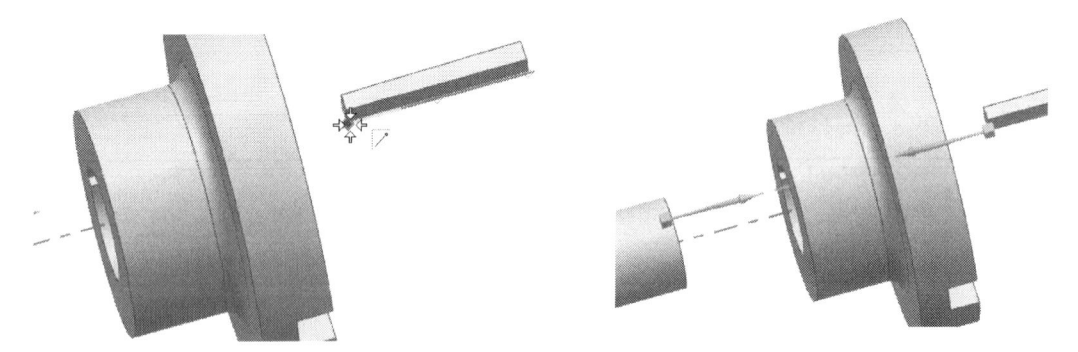

12. Click **OK** to create the traceline.

13. Create tracelines between rest of the parts.

14. Change the view to **Wireframe with Hidden Edges**.

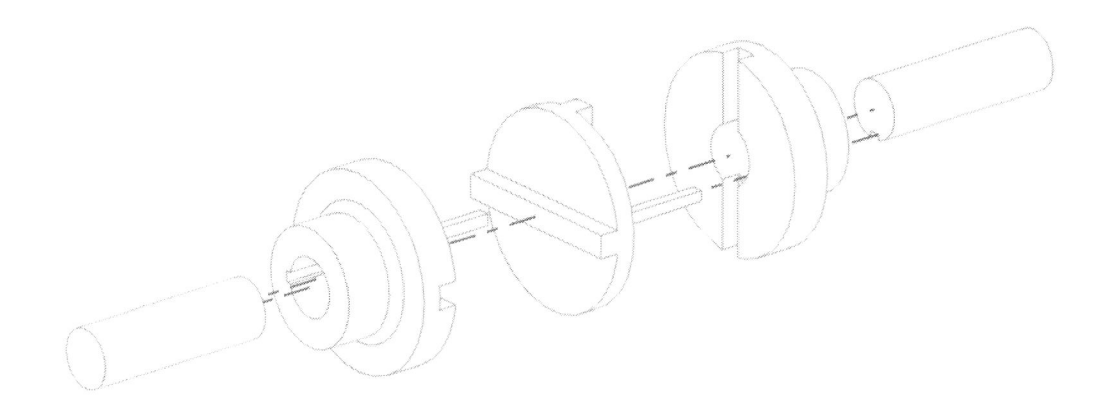

15. Click **Save** on the **Standard** toolbar, or click **File > Save**.

4

Creating Drawings

In this chapter, you create drawings of the parts and assembly from previous chapters.

In this chapter, you will:
- *Open and editing a drawing template*
- *Insert standard views of a part model*
- *Add model and reference annotations*
- *Add another drawing sheet*
- *Insert exploded view of the assembly*
- *Insert a bill of materials of the assembly*
- *Apply balloons to the assembly*

TUTORIAL 1

In this tutorial, you will create drawings of parts created in previous chapters.

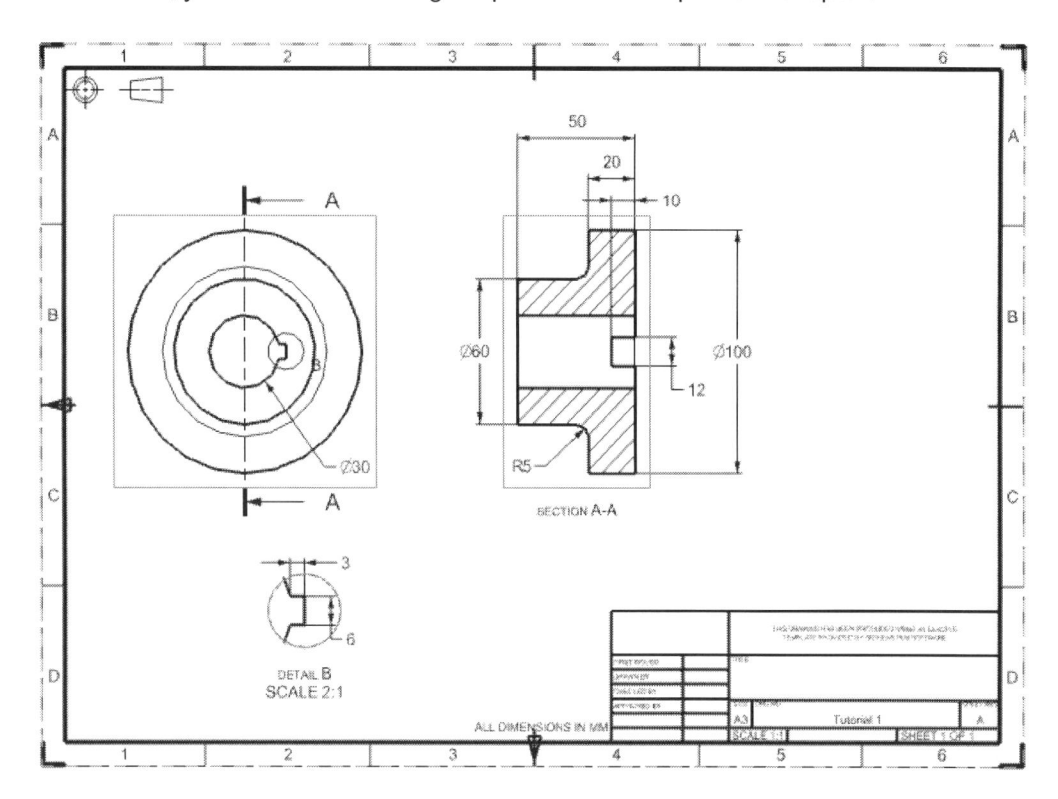

Creating a New Drawing File

1. To create a new drawing, click the **New** button on the **Standard** toolbar, or click **File > New** on the menu bar; the **New** dialog box appears.

2. Select the **Drawing** tab

3 Click **A3-Size** in the **Template** group.

4. Click **OK**; a new drawing window appears. Also, the **Populate Title Block** dialog box appears.

5. Click **Close** button on this dialog box.

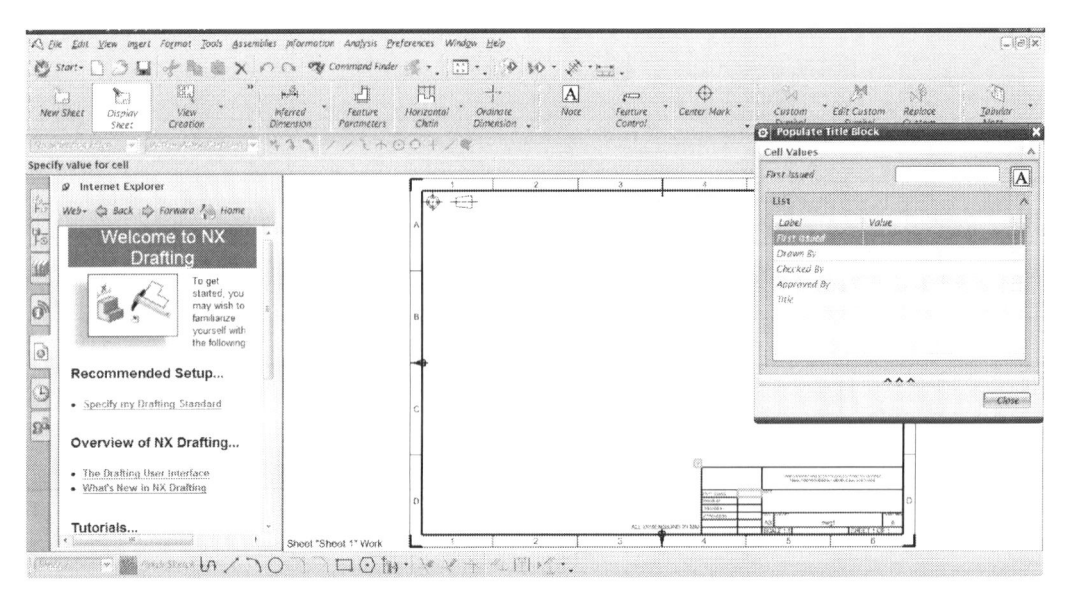

Editing the Drawing Sheet
1. To edit the drawing sheet, click **Edit Sheet** button on the **Drafting Edit** toolbar, or click **Edit > Sheet** on the menu bar; the **Sheet** dialog box appears.

2. Click the **More** button (three down-arrows) displayed at the bottom of the dialog box; the **Settings** group appears.

3. Set **Millimeters** as Units.

4. Set the **Projection** type to **Third Angle Projection**.

5. Click **OK** on the **Sheet** dialog box to create a new sheet.

Generating the Base View
1. To generate the base view, click **Base** button from the **Add View** drop-down on the **Drawing** toolbar, or click **Insert > View > Base** on the menu bar; the **Base View** message box appears.

2. Click **Yes** on the message box; the **Part Name** dialog box appears.

3. Browse to the location NX8.5/C3/Oldham_Coupling and double-click on **Flange.prt**; the **Base View** dialog box appears.

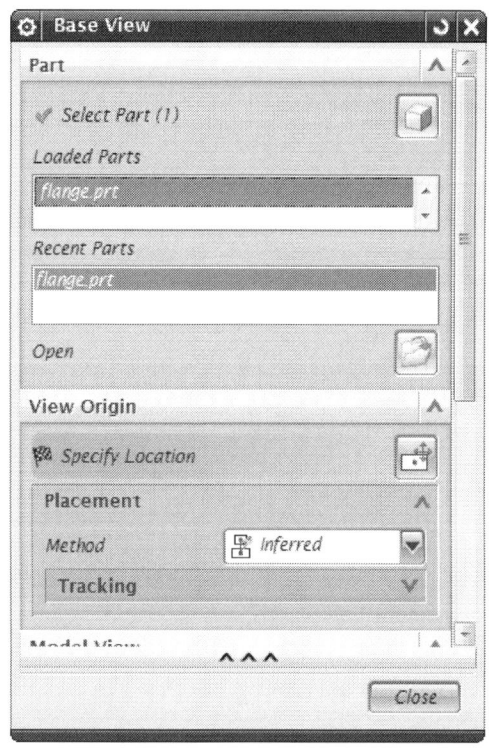

Also, the view is attached to the cursor.

4. Select **Front** from the **Model View to Use** drop-down in the **Mode View** group.

5. Place the view as shown in figure; the **Projected View** dialog box appears.

6. Click **Close** to close the dialog box.

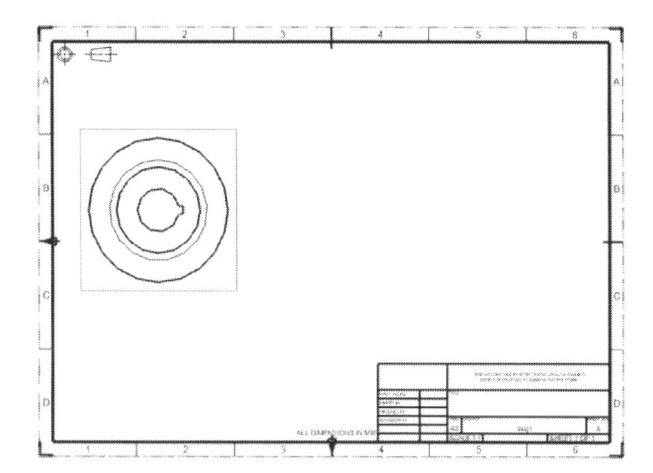

Creating the Section View

1. To create the section view, click **Section View** button from the **Add View** drop-down on the **Drawing** toolbar, or click **Insert > View > Section > Simple/ Stepped** on the menu bar; the **Section View** dialog bar appears.

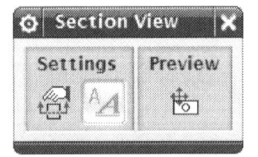

2. Select the base view; the section line is attached to the cursor.

3. Click on the center point of the base view.

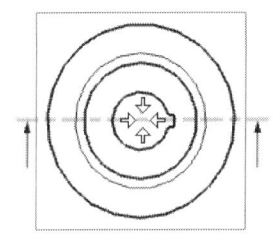

4. Move the cursor toward right and click to place the section view.

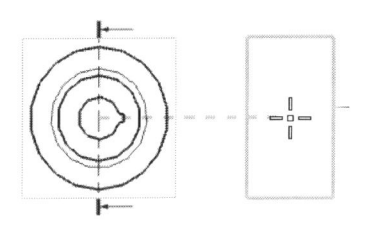

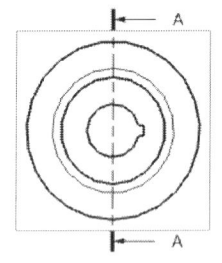

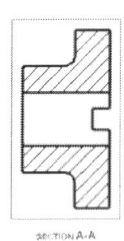

Creating the Detailed View

Now, you need to create the detailed view of the keyway which is displayed in the front view.

1. To create the detailed view, click **Detail View** button from the **Add View** drop-down on the **Drawing** toolbar, or click **Insert > View > Detail** on the menu bar; the **Detail View** dialog box appears.

2. Select **Circular** from the **Type** drop-down.

3. Select **2:1** from the **Scale** drop-down.

4. Specify the center point and boundary point of the detail view as show figure.

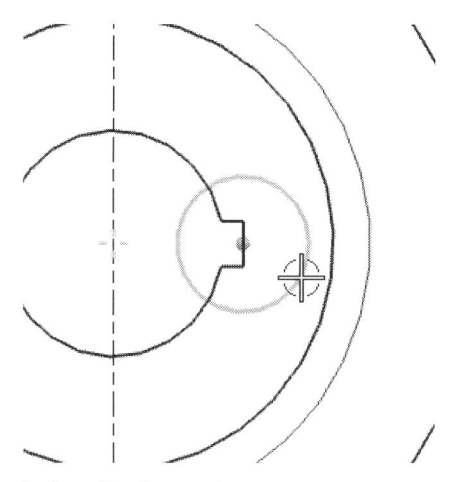

5. Place the detail view below the base view.

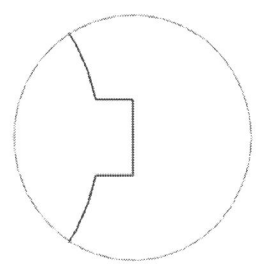

DETAIL B
SCALE 2:1

Specifying Dimension Settings
1. To specify the dimension settings, click **Preference >Annotation** on the menu bar; the **Annotation Preferences** dialog box appears.

2. Click the **Dimension** tab.

3. Select **Horizontal** from the **Alignment** drop-down.

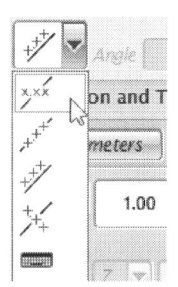

4. Select **No Leader** from the drop-down in the **Narrow** group.

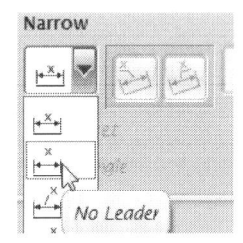

5. Enter 2 in the **Text Offset** edit box in the **Narrow** group.

6. Click the **Line/Arrow** tab.

7. Enter 5 in the **A** edit box.

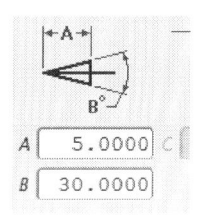

8. Click the **Lettering** tab.

9. Enter 5 in the **Character Size** edit box.

10. Click **OK**.

Generate Feature Dimensions

Now, you generate dimensions that were applied to the model while creating it.

1. To generate dimensions, click **Feature Parameters** button on the **Dimension** toolbar, or click **Insert > Dimension > Feature Parameters** on the menu bar; the **Feature Parameters** dialog box appears.

2. Click on the + symbol next to **flange**; the **FEATURES** node appears.

3. Expand the **FEATURES** node.

4. Press Ctrl key and select all the sketches under it.

5. Click **Select Views** button on the **Feature Parameters** dialog box.

6. Select the section view on the drawing sheet.

7. Click **OK** to generate feature dimensions.

SECTION A-A

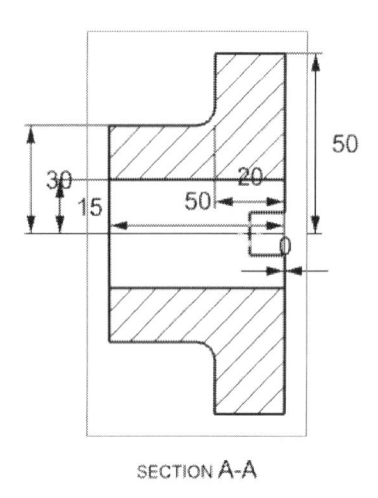

8. Delete the unwanted dimension and arrange the required dimensions as shown in figure.

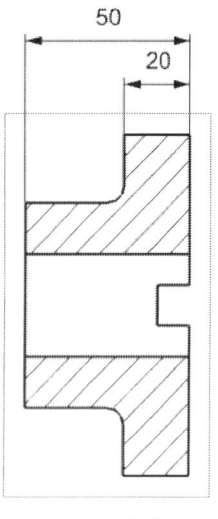

SECTION A-A

Tip:
- Select the dimensions and press the Delete key to delete the dimensions.
- Click on the required dimension and drag the cursor to arrange the dimensions.

Adding additional dimensions

1. To add dimensions, click **Cylinder Dimension** button on the **Dimension** toolbar, or click **Insert > Dimension > Cylinder** on the menu bar; the **Cylinder Dimension** dialog bar appears.

2. Create the two dimensions as shown in figure.

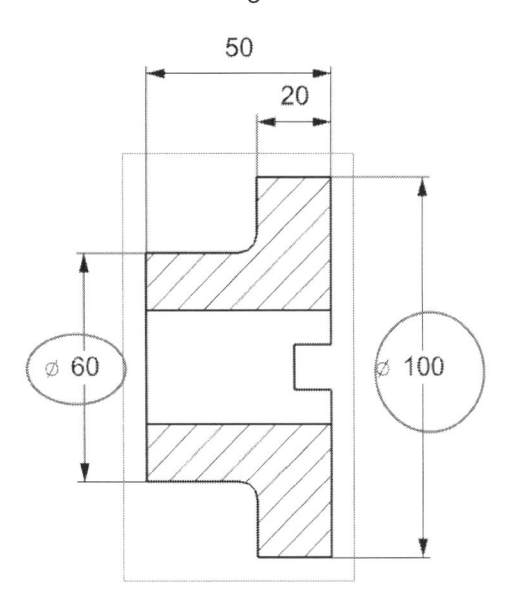

3. Click **Inferred Dimension** button on the **Dimension** toolbar, or click **Insert > Dimension > Inferred** on the menu bar; the **Inferred Dimension** dialog bar appears.

4. Create the remaining dimensions on the section view as shown in figure.

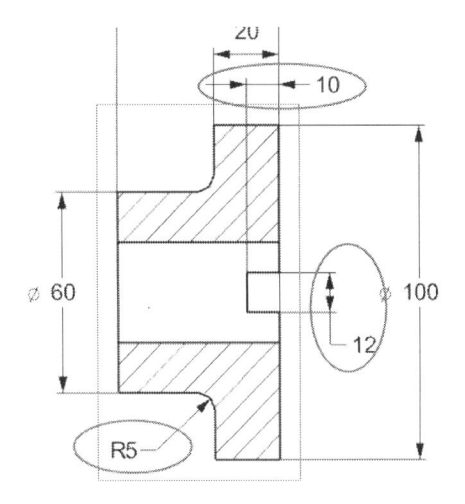

5. Click **Hole Dimension** button on the **Dimension** toolbar, or click **Insert > Dimension > Hole** on the menu bar; the **Hole Dimension** dialog bar appears.

6. Create the hole dimension on the front view as shown in figure.

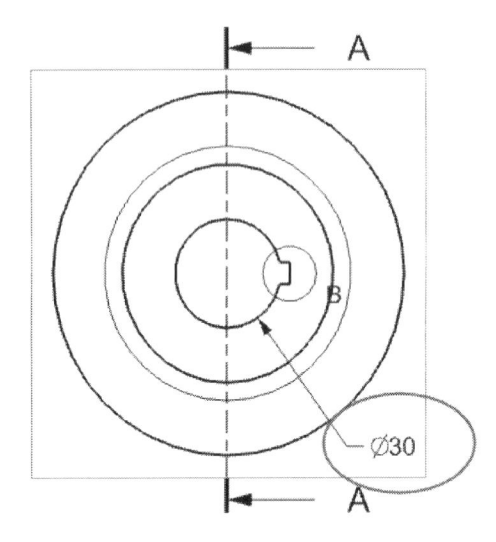

7. Click **Inferred Dimension** on the **Dimension** toolbar.

8. Create the dimensions on the detail view as shown in figure.

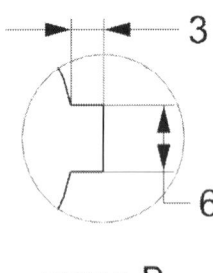

Saving the Drawing

1. Click **Save** on the **Standard** toolbar, or click **File > Save**; the **Name Parts** dialog box appears.

2. Specify **Tutorial 1** as **Name** and click **Folder** button.

3. Browse to NX 8.5/C3 folder and then click **OK** button twice.

Adding another Sheet
Now you create an additional drawing sheet for the Disc.prt.

1. To add a new sheet, click **New Sheet** button on the **Drawing** toolbar, or click **Insert > Sheet**.

2. Select **Template** radio button.

3. Select **A3 -Size** from the **Size** list box.

4. Click **OK** on the **Sheet** dialog box to create a new sheet.

5. Click **Close** to close the **Populate** dialog box.

Generating Drawing Views
1. To generate views, click **View Creation Wizard** button on the **Drawing** toolbar, or click **Insert > View > View Creation Wizard** on the menu bar; the **View Creation Wizard** dialog box appears.

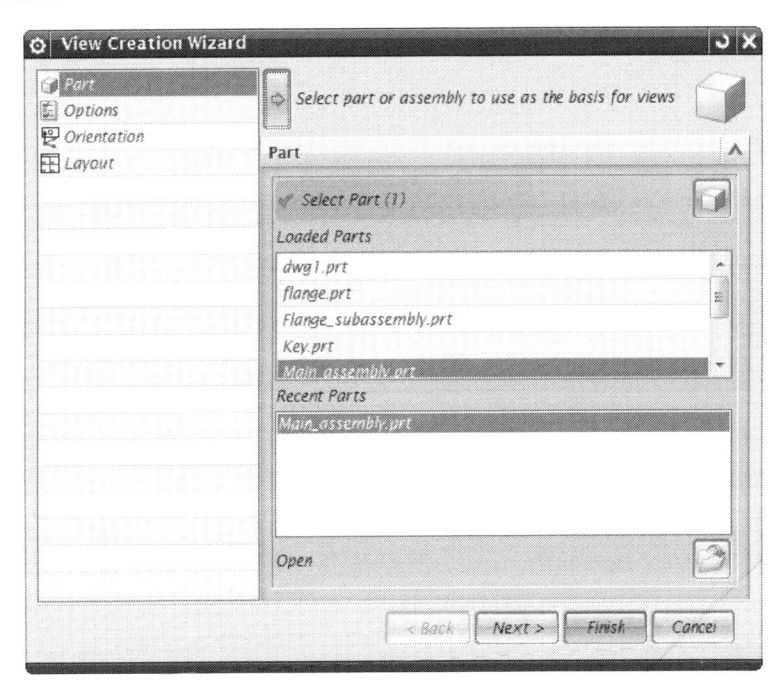

4-13   Creating Drawings

2. Click the **Open** button on the **View Creation Wizard**.

3. Browse to the location NX8.5/C3/Oldham_Coupling and double-click on **Disc.prt**; the **View Creation Wizard** appears.

4. Click **Next**; the **Options** page appears in the **View Creation Wizard**.

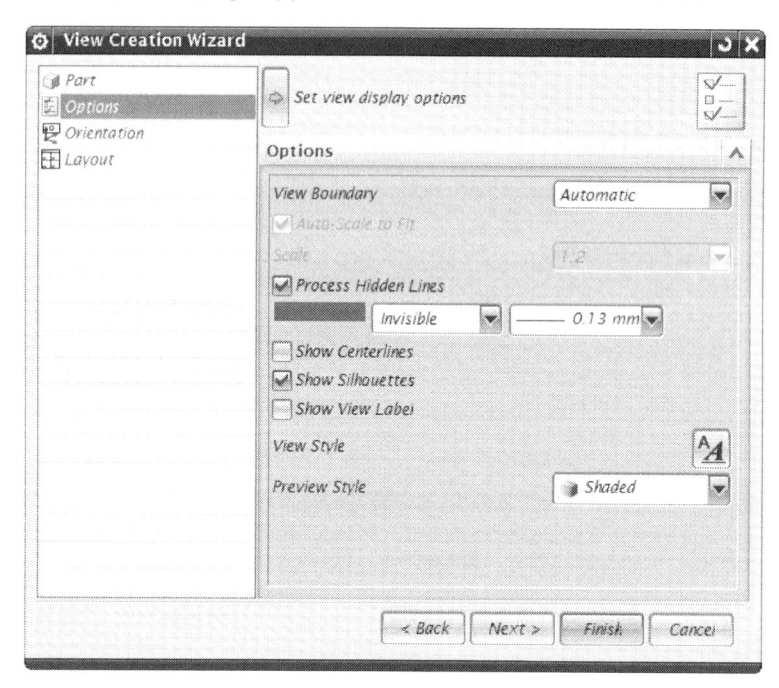

5. Select **Manual** from the **View Boundary** drop-down.

6. Clear the **Auto-Scale to Fit** check box.

7. Select **1:1** from the Scale drop-down.

8. Select **Dashed** from the **Hidden Lines** drop-down.

9. Click **Next**; the **Orientation** page appears.

10. Select **Front** and then click **Next**; the **Layout** page appears.

11. Select the views as shown in figure.

Views to be selected

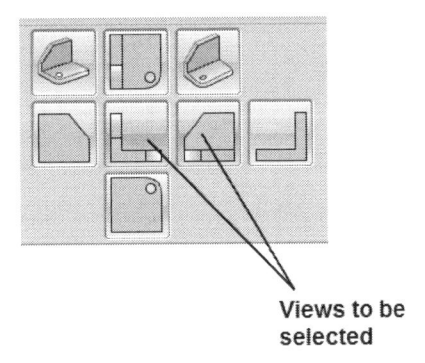

12. Select **Manual** from the **Option** drop-down.

13. Specify the center of the views as shown figure.

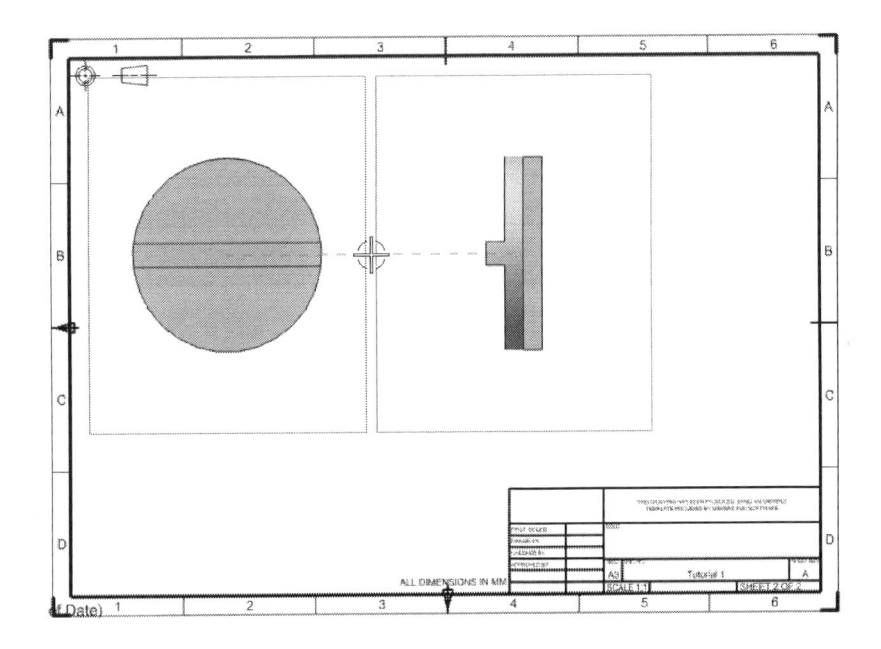

Generating Dimensions
1. Generate dimensions on the front view using the **Feature Parameters** tool.

Creating Drawings   4-15

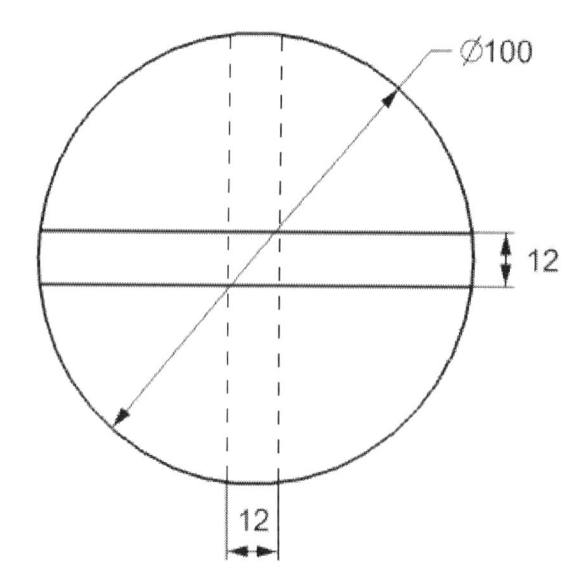

Now, you create horizontal chain dimensions on the right-side view.

2. Click the **Horizontal Chain** button on the **Dimension** toolbar, or click **Insert > Dimension > Horizontal Chain** on the menu bar; the **Horizontal Chain Dimension** dialog bar appears.

3. Select the end points on the right-side view in the sequence, as shown in figure.

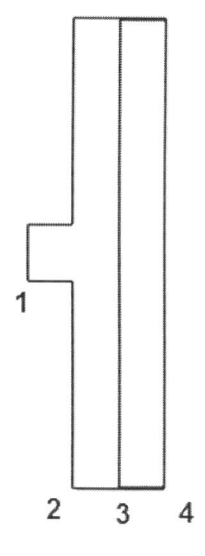

4. Place the chain dimension as shown in figure.

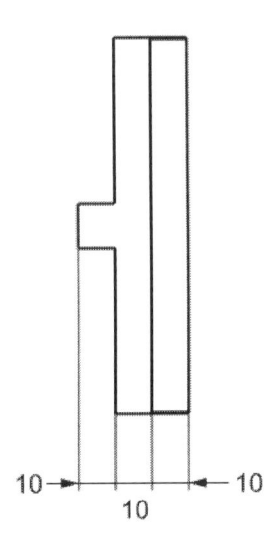

Saving the Drawing

1. Click **Save** on the **Standard** toolbar, or click **File > Save**.

2. Click **File > Close > All Parts**.

TUTORIAL 2
In this tutorial, you will create drawing Oldham coupling assembly created in the previous chapter.

Opening the Assembly file
1. To open the assembly file, click the **Open** button on the **Standard** toolbar, or click **File > Open** on the menu bar; the **Open** dialog box appears.

2. Browse to the location NX8.5/C3/Oldham_Coupling and double-click on **Main_assembly.prt**.

Starting the Drawing Environment
1. To start the drawing environment, click **Start > Drafting** on the **Standard** toolbar; the **Sheet** dialog box appears.

4-17   Creating Drawings

2. Select **Standard Size** from the **Size** group.

3. Select **A3-297 x 420** from the **Size** drop-down.

4. Select **1:2** from the **Scale** drop-down.

5. Click the **More** button (three down-arrows) displayed at the bottom of the dialog box; the **Settings** group appears.

6. Set **Units** to **Millimeters**.

7. Select **Base View Command**.

8. Click **OK**; the **Base View** dialog box appears.

9. Select **Isometric** from the **Model View to Use** drop-down in the **Model View** group.

10. Click in the left side of the drawing sheet; the **Projected View** dialog box appears.

11. Click **Close**.

Creating the Exploded View

1. Click the **Base View** button on the **Drawing** toolbar, or click **Insert > View > Base** on the menu bar; the **Base View** dialog box appears.

2. Select **Trimetric** from the **Model View to Use** drop-down.

3. Click in the right side of the drawing sheet; the **Projected View** dialog box appears.

4. Click **Close**.

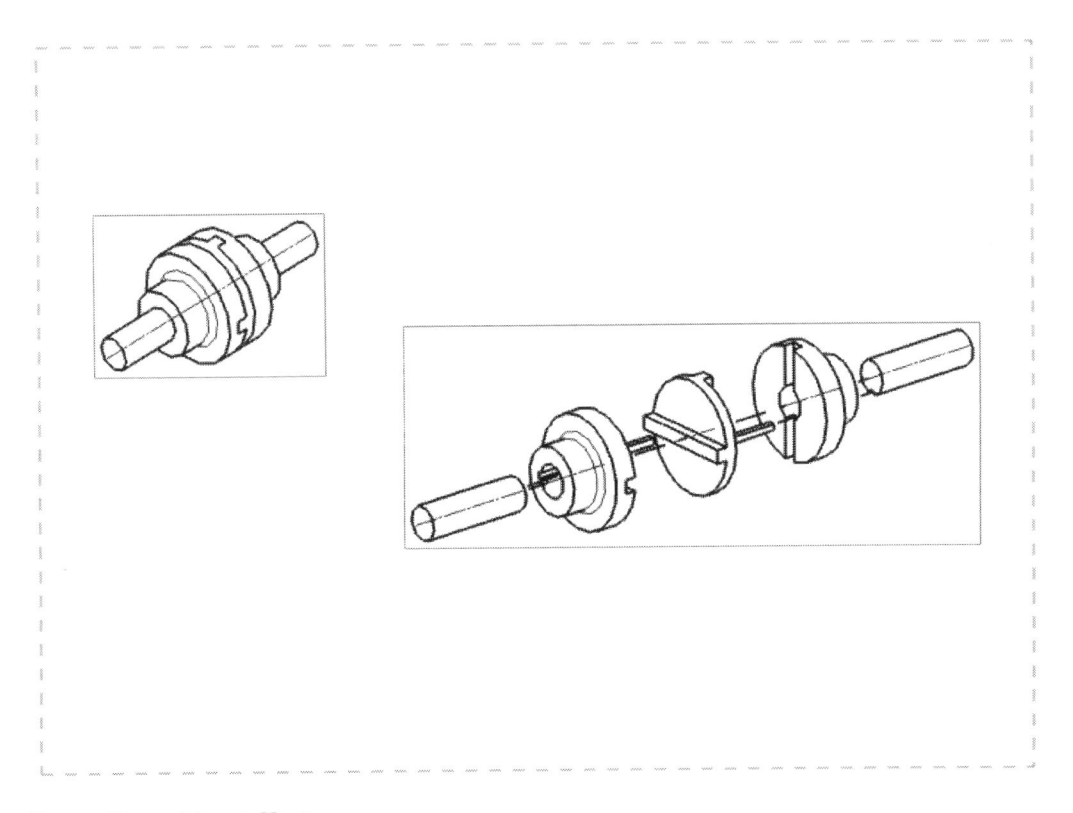

Creating Part list.
1. To create a part list, click the **Part List** button on the **Table** toolbar, or click **Insert > Table > Part List** on the menu bar.

2. Place the part list at the top-right corner.

Creating Balloons
1. To create balloons, click the **Auto Balloon** button on the **Table** toolbar, or click **Insert > Table > Auto Balloon** on the menu bar; the **Part List Auto-Balloon** dialog box appears.

2. Select the part list.

3. Click OK.

4. Select **Isometric@1** from the **Part List Auto-Balloon** dialog box.

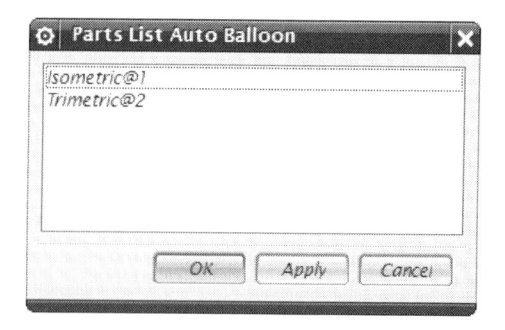

5. Click **OK** to create balloons.

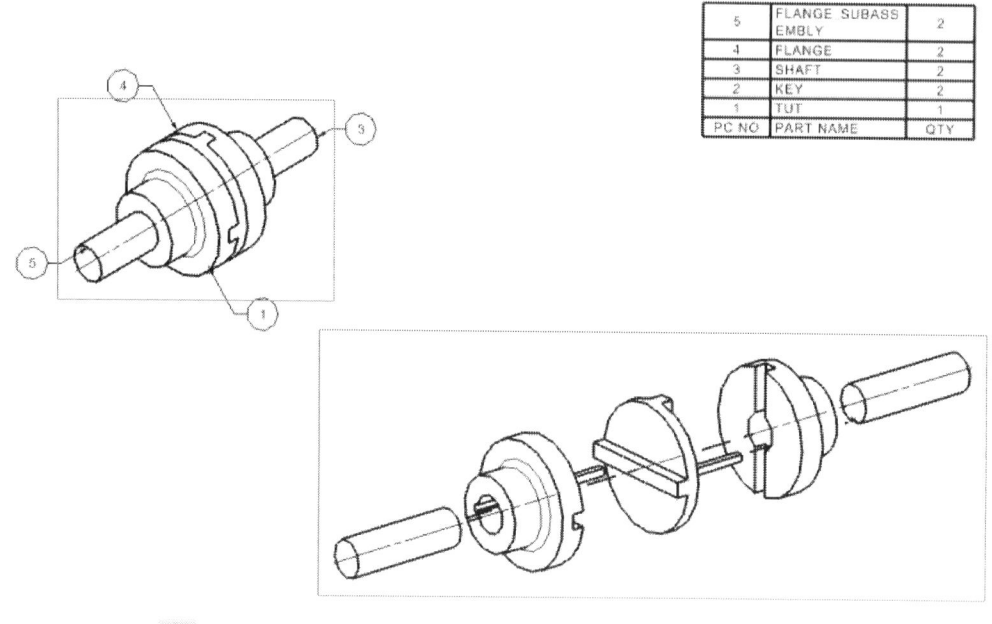

6. Click **Save** on the **Standard** toolbar,

5

Additional Modeling Tools

In this chapter, you create models using additional modeling tools.

In this chapter, you will:
- Create a Sweep feature
- Create a Swept feature along guide curves
- Create Holes
- Create Grooves and Slots
- Create Pattern Features
- Create Tube features
- Create Instance Geometry
- Apply Boolean operations
- Create chamfers

TUTORIAL 1

In this tutorial, you will create a helical spring using the **Helix** and **Sweep along Guide** tools.

Creating the Helix

1. Open a NX file using the **Model** template.

2. To create a helix, click **Insert > Curve > Helix** on the menu bar; the **Helix** dialog box appears.

3. Select **Along Vector** from the **Type** dropd-down.

4. Select the coordinate system from the graphics window.

5. Specify the settings in the **Size** group as given next.

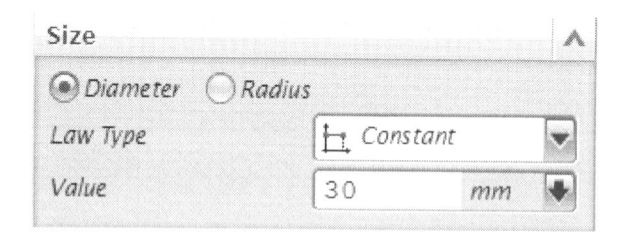

6. Specify the settings in the **Pitch** group as given next.

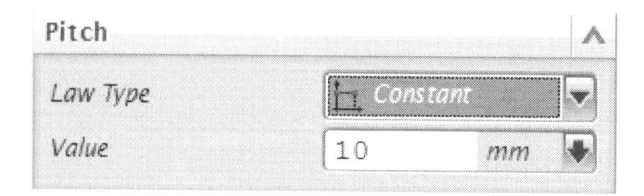

7. Specify the settings in the **Line** group as given next.

Additional Modeling Tools

Length	
Method	Turns
Turns	10

8. Expand the dialog box and specify the settings in the **Settings** group as given next.

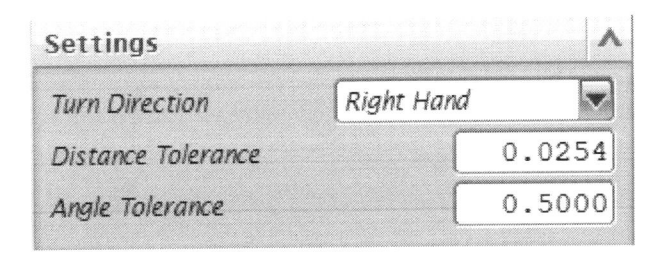

Settings	
Turn Direction	Right Hand
Distance Tolerance	0.0254
Angle Tolerance	0.5000

9. Click **OK** to create the helix.

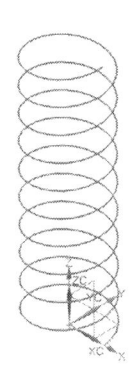

Creating the Datum Plane

1. To create a datum plane, click **Datum Plane** button on the **Feature** toolbar, or click **Insert > Datum Point > Datum Plane** on the menu bar; the **Datum Plane** dialog box appears.

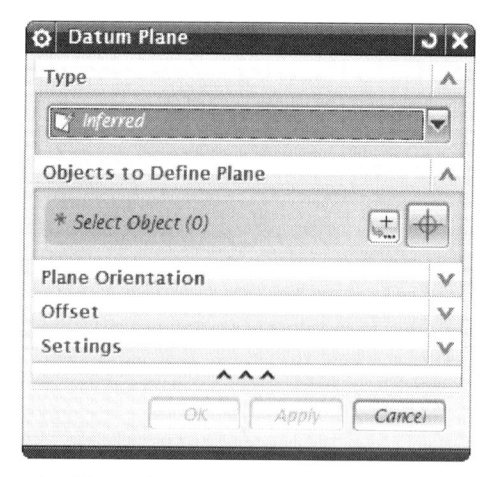

2. Select **On Curve** from the **Type** drop-down.

3. Select the helix from the graphics window.

4. Select **Through Curve** from the **Location** drop-down.

5. Select the end point of the helix.

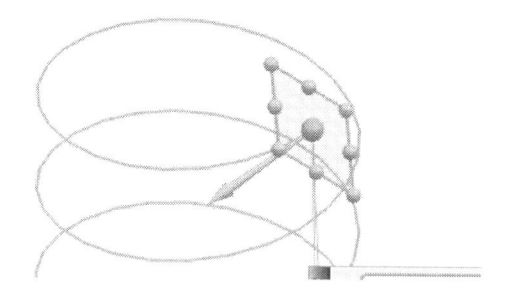

6. Select **Normal to path** from the **Orientation on Curve** group.

7. Leave the default values and click OK.

Creating the Sweep feature

1. Click the **Sketch** button on the **Direct Sketch** toolbar.

2. Select the plane created normal to helix.

3. Draw circle of 4 mm diameter.

Additional Modeling Tools

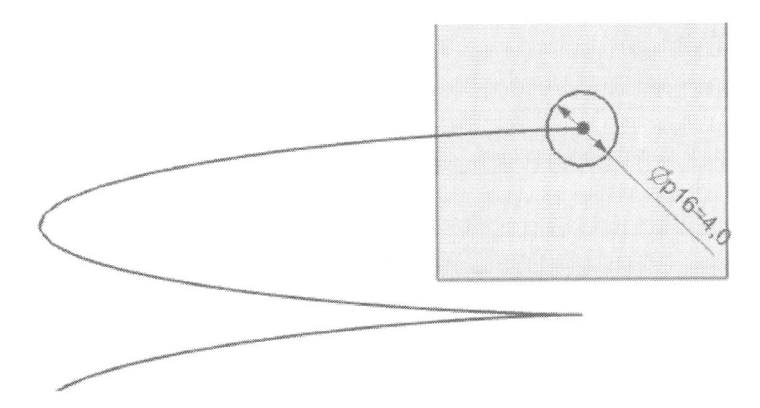

5. Right-click and select **Finish Sketch.**

6. Click the **Isometric** button from the **Orient View** drop-down on the **View** toolbar.

7. To create a sweep feature, click **Insert > Sweep > Sweep along Guide** on the menu bar; the **Sweep Along Guide** dialog box appears.

8. Select the circle created in the previous sketch.

9. Click **Select Curve** in the **Guide** group.

10. Select the helix.

11. Leave the default settings and click **OK** to create the sweep feature.

12. Right-click on the plane and select **Hide**.

    Also, hide the sketches.

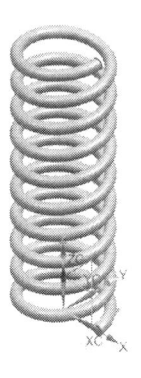

13. Save and close the file.

TUTORIAL 2

In this tutorial, you create a pulley wheel using the **Revolve** and **Groove** tools.

1. Open a file in the Modeling Environment.

2. Create the sketch on the YZ plane as shown in figure.

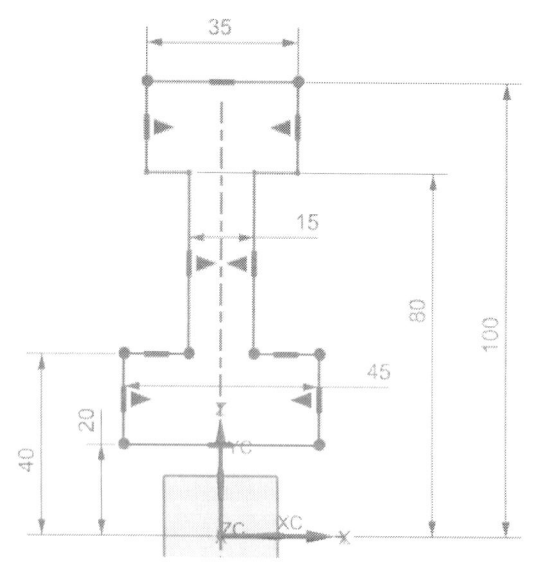

3. Create the revolved feature.

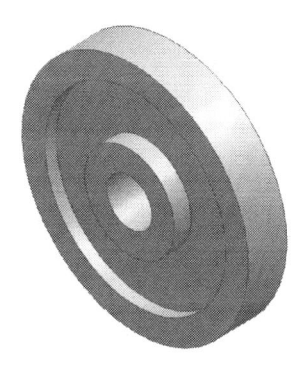

Creating the Groove feature

1. To create a groove feature, click the **Groove** button on the **Feature** toolbar, or click **Insert > Design Feature > Groove** on the menu bar; the **Groove** dialog box appears.

Note
Some tools are not displayed on the toolbar. To displayed the required tools, customize the toolbar as shown in figure.

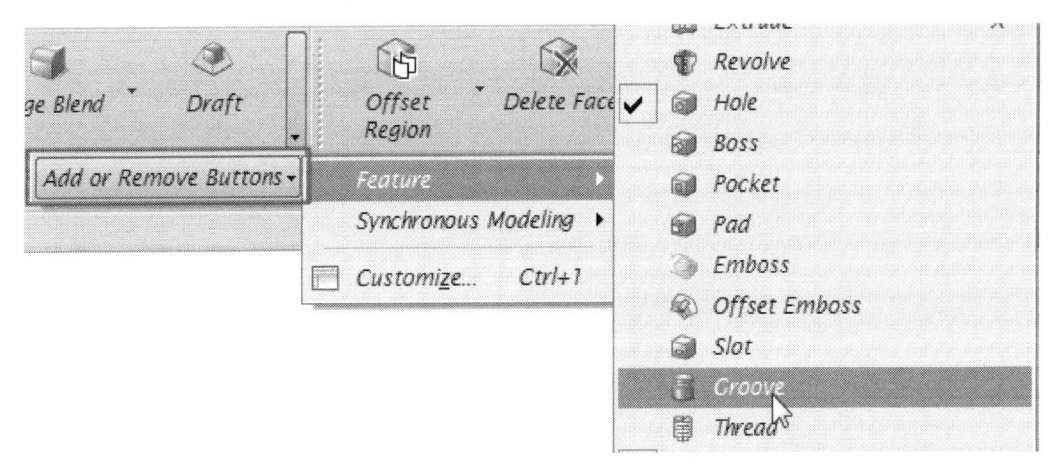

2. Click the **U Groove** button on the dialog box.

3. Select the outer cylindrical face of the base feature.

4. Specify the values in the groove edit box as shown in figure.

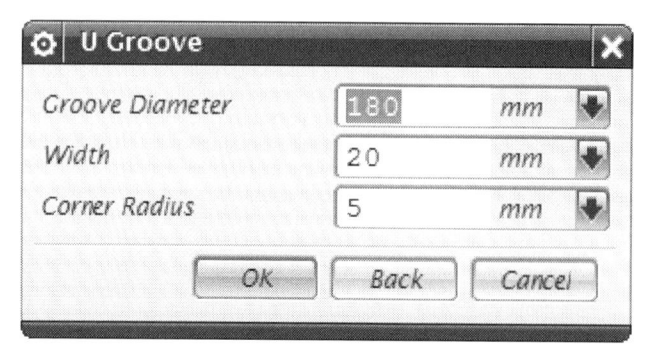

5. Click OK; the **Position Groove** dialog box appears.

6. Select the cylindrical edges on the model and groove preview.

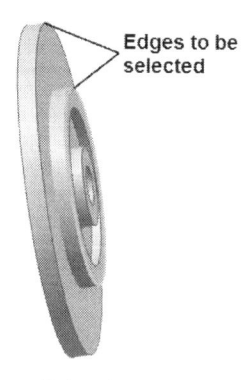

7. Enterr **7.5 mm** in the **Expression** dialog box.

8. Click **OK** to create the groove.

9. Click **Cancel** to exit the tool.

10. Save and close the model.

TUTORIAL 3

In this tutorial, you create a shampoo bottle using the **Swept**, **Extrude**, and **Thread** tools.

Creating Sections and Guide curves

To create a swept feature, you need to create sections and guide curves.

1. Open a file in the Modeling Environment.

2. Click the **Sketch** button on the **Direct Sketch** toolbar.

3. Select the XY plane.

4. Click the **Ellipse** button on the **Direct Sketch** toolbar, or click **Insert > Sketch Curve > Ellipse** on the menu bar; the **Ellipse** dialog box appears.

5. Select the origin point of the coordinate system.

6. Specify **Major Radius** as 50 mm.

7. Specify **Minor Radius** as 20 mm.

8. Leave the default settings and click OK.

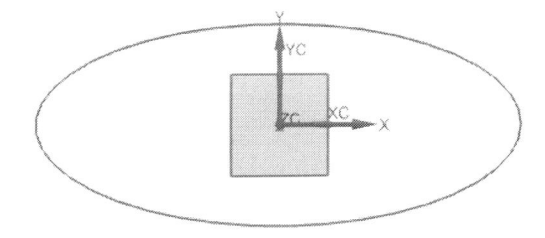

9. Click **Finish Sketch**.

10. Change the orientation to Isometric.

11. Click the **Sketch** button on the **Direct Sketch** toolbar.

12. Select the XZ plane.

13. Click the **Studio Spline** button on the **Direct Sketch** toolbar, or click **Insert > Sketch Curve > Studio Spline** on the menu bar; the **Studio Spline** dialog box appears.

14. Select **Through Points** option from the **Type** drop-down.

15. Create a spline similarly to the one shown in figure.

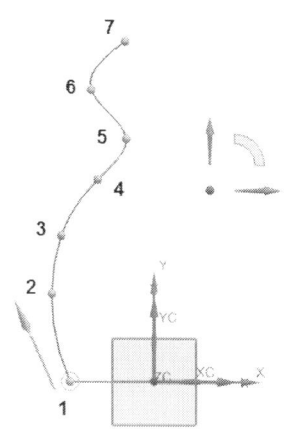

Ensure that the first point of the spline coincides with the previous sketch.

16. Apply dimension to the spline, as shown in figure.

Additional Modeling Tools

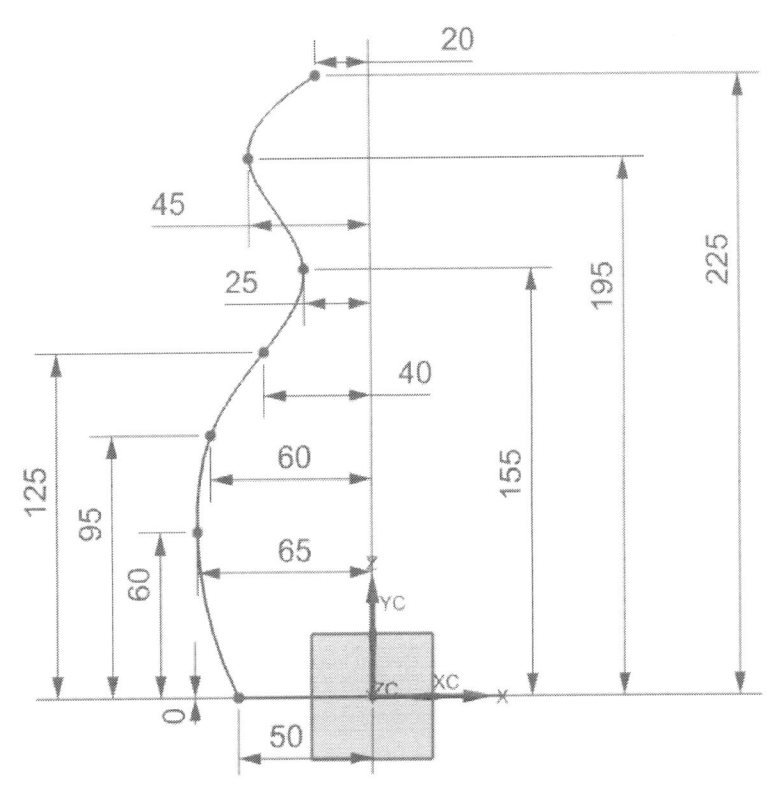

17. Click the **Mirror Curve** button on the **Direct Sketch** toolbar, or click **Insert > Sketch Curve > Mirror Curve** on the menu bar; the **Mirror Curve** dialog box appears.

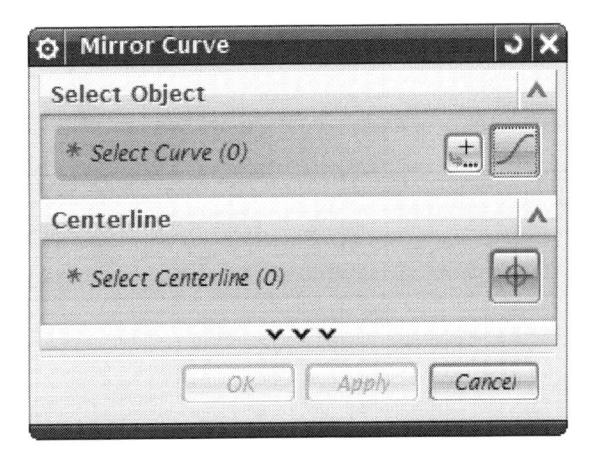

18. Select the spline.

19. Click **Select Centerline** on the **Mirror Curve** dialog box and then select the vertical axis of the sketch.

20. Click OK.

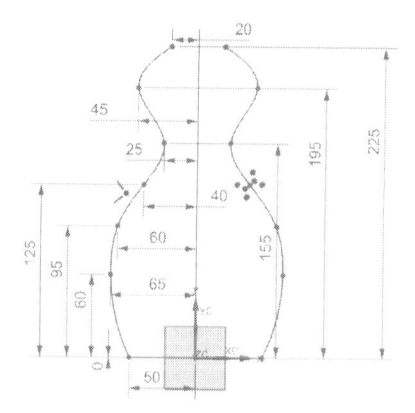

21. Click **Finish Sketch**.

22. Change the view orientation to Isometric.

Creating the second section

1. Click **Datum Plane** button on the **Feature** toolbar, or click **Insert > Datum Point > Datum Plane** on the menu bar; the **Datum Plane** dialog box appears.

2. Select **At Distance** option from the **Type** drop-down.

3. Select the XY plane from the coordinate system.

4. Enter **225** in the **Distance** edit box.

5. Click OK.

6. Start a sketch on the newly created datum plane.

7. Create a circle of 40 mm diameter.

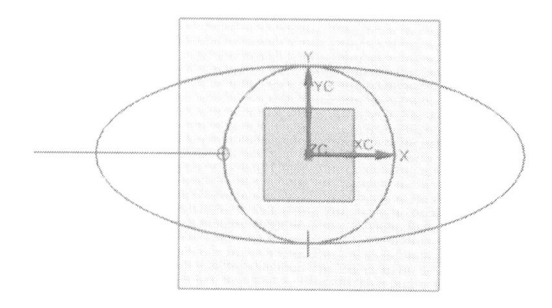

8. Click **Finish Sketch**.

9. Change the view to Isometric.

Creating the swept feature

1. To create a swept feature, click **Insert > Sweep > Swept** on the menu bar; the **Swept** dialog box appears.

2. Select the circle and click the middle mouse button.

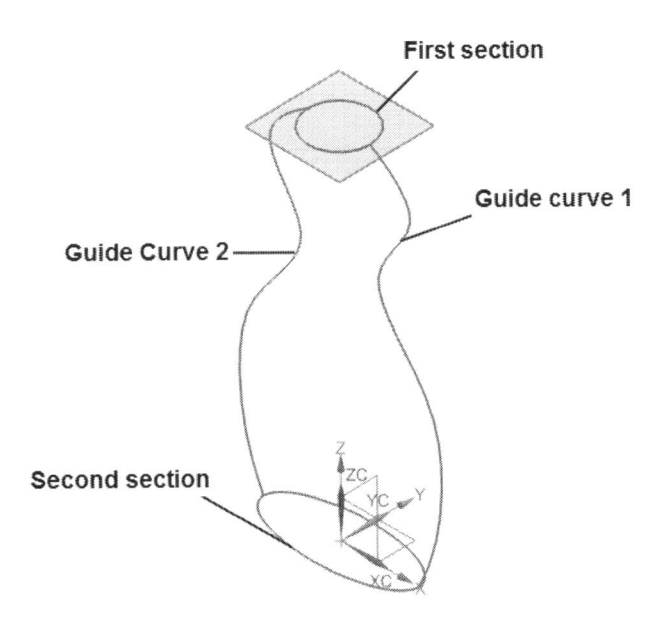

3. Select the ellipse.

   Ensure that the arrows on the circle and the ellipse point towards same direction. Use the **Reverse Direction** button in the Section group to reverse the direction of arrows.

4. Click **Select Curve** in the **Guides (3 maximum)** group.

5. Select the first guide curve and click the middle mouse button.

6. Select the second guide curve.

7. Click **OK** to create the swept feature.

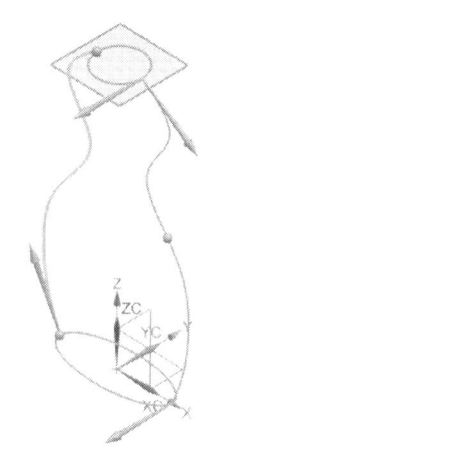

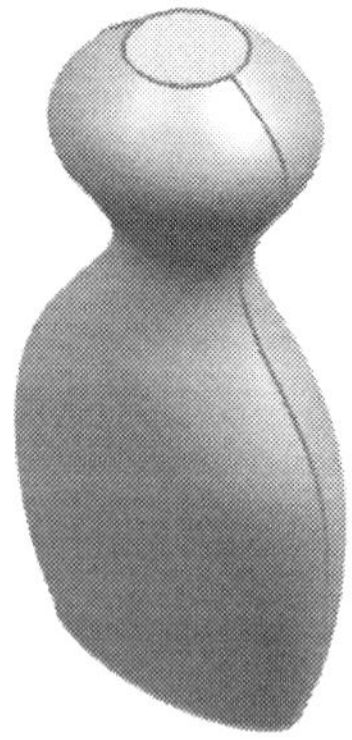

Creating the Extruded feature

1. Click on the circle on the top of the sweep feature.

2. Click the **Extrude** button on the contextual toolbar.

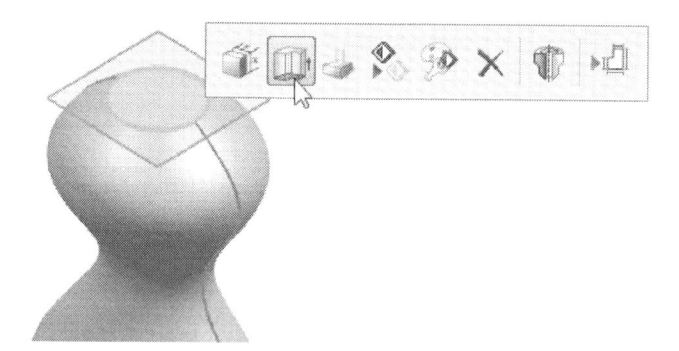

3. Extrude the circle upto 25 mm.

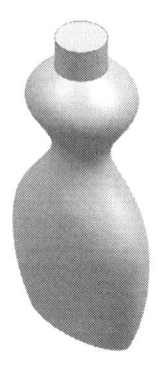

Creating the Emboss feature

1. Click the **Datum Plane** button on the **Feature** toolbar.

2. Select **At Distance** from the **Type** drop-down.

3. Select the XZ plane from the coordinate system.

4. Enter **50** in the **Distance** edit box.

5. Create a sketch on the plane as shown in figure. The major and minor radius of the ellipse are 50 and 20, respectively

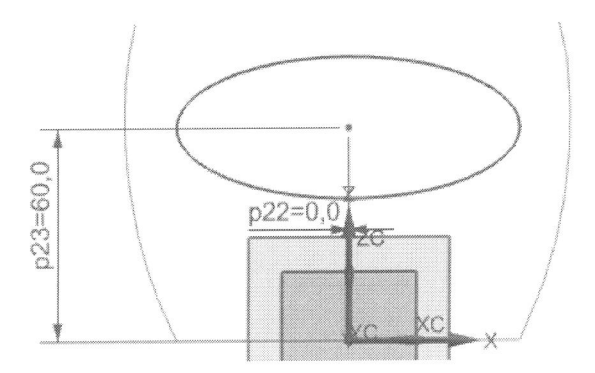

6. Click **Finish Sketch**.

7. Click the **Emboss** button on the **Feature** toolbar, or click **Insert > Design Feature > Emboss** on the menu bar; the **Emboss** dialog box appears.

8. Select the sketch.

9. Select the swept feature.

10. Specify the settings in the **End Cap** group as given in figure.

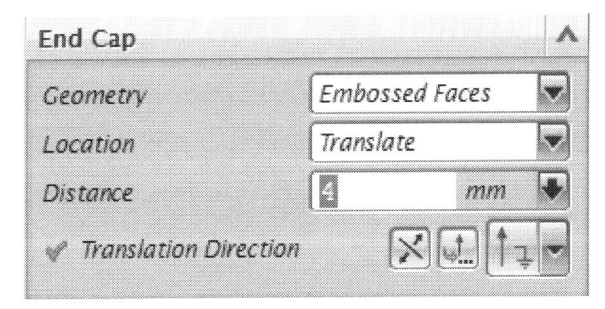

11. Leave the default settings and click **OK** to create the embossed feature.

Creating Edge Blend

1. Click **Edge Blend** on the **Feature** toolbar, or click **Insert > Detail Feature > Edge Blend**; the **Edge Blend** dialog box appears.

2. Click on the bottom and top edges of the swept feature.

3. Set **Radius 1** as 5 mm

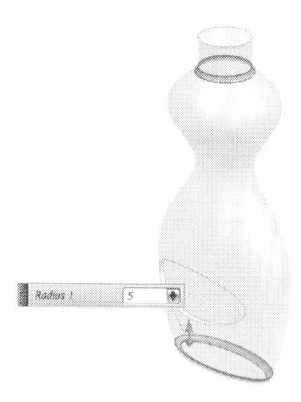

4. Click **Apply** to add the blend.

5. Set **Radius 1** as 1 mm.

6. Select the edges of the emboss feature and click **OK**.

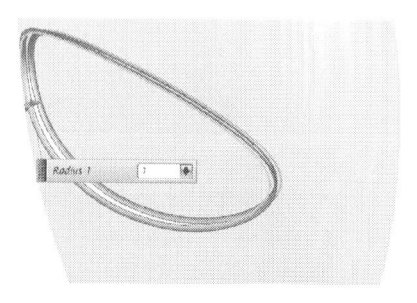

Shelling the Model

1. Click **Shell** on the **Feature** toolbar, or click **Insert > Offset/Scale > Shell**; the **Shell** dialog box appears.

2. Set **Thickness** as 2 mm.

3. Select the top face of the cylindrical feature.

4. Click OK to create the shell.

Creating Threads

1. Click **Thread** on the **Feature** toolbar, or click **Insert > Design Feature > Thread**; the **Thread** dialog box appears.

2. Select **Detailed** from the **Thread** dialog box.

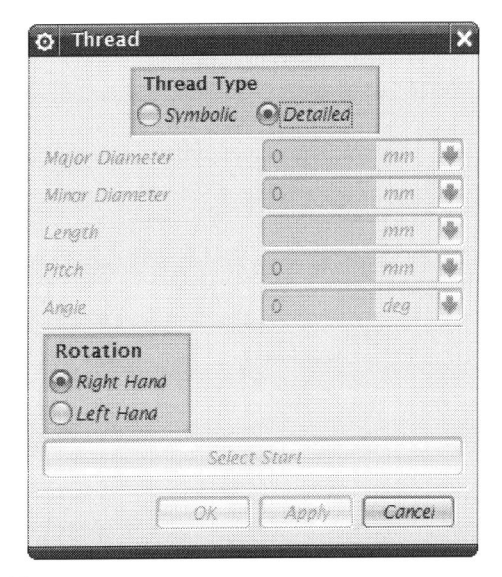

3. Select the cylindrical face.

4. Set **Pitch** as 8 mm.

5. Leave the other default settings and click **OK** to create the thread.

6. Save the model and close it.

TUTORIAL 4
In this tutorial, you create a patterned cylindrical shell.

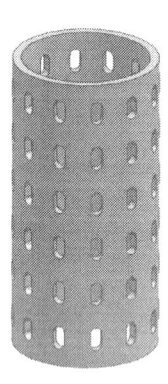

Creating a cylindrical shell
1. To create a cylindrical feature, or click **Insert > Design Feature > Cylinder**; the **Cylinder** dialog box appears.

   Also, a triad is displayed in the graphics window.

Additional Modeling Tools

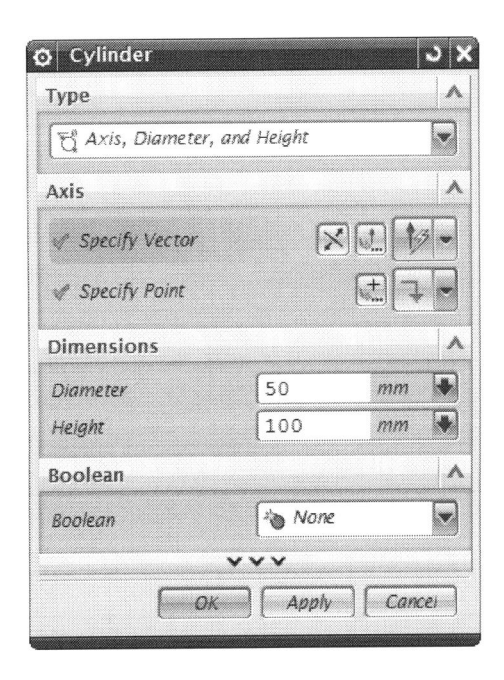

2. Select **Axis, Diameter, and Height** from the **Type** drop-down.

3. Select the Z-axis from the triad.

4. Specify **Diameter** and **Height** as **50** and **100**, respectively.

5. Leave the default settings and click OK.

6. Click **Shell** on the **Feature** toolbar, or click **Insert > Offset/Scale > Shell**; the **Shell** dialog box appears.

7. Set **Thickness** as 3 mm.

8. Select the top and bottom faces of the cylindrical feature.

9. Click OK to create the shell.

Creating slots

1. Click **Slot** on the **Feature** toolbar, or click **Insert > Design Feature > Slot**; the **Slot** dialog box appears.

2. Select **Rectangle** from the **Slot** dialog box and then click **OK**.

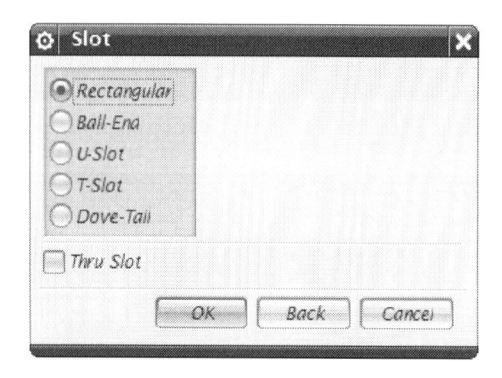

3. Click on the YZ plane.

4. Click **Flip Default Side**.

5. Select Z-axis from the Datum Coordinate System.

6. Specify 8, 4, and 30 as **Length**, **Width** and **Depth**, respectively.

7. Click **OK**; the **Positioning** dialog box appears. Also, the slot tool appears.

8. Click the **Horizontal** button on the **Positioning** dialog box.

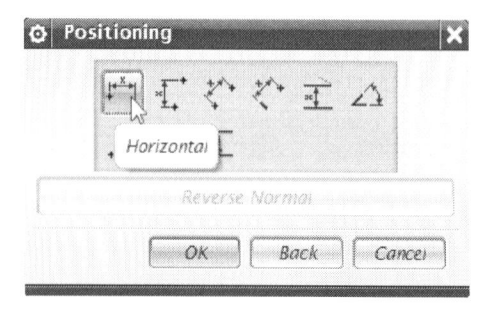

9. Select the circular edge of the cylindrical feature; the **Set Arc Position** dialog box appears.

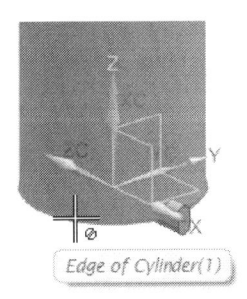

10. Click **Arc Center** on the dialog box.

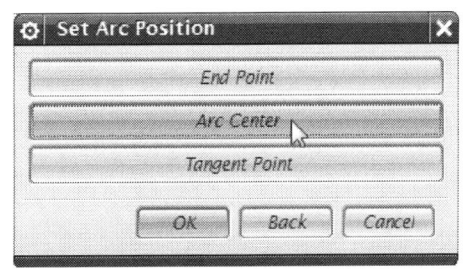

11. Select the circular edge on the slot tool; the **Set Arc Position** dialog box appears.

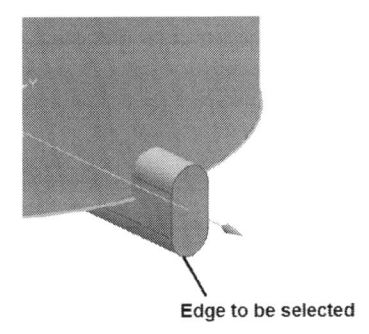

12. Click **Arc Center** on the dialog box; the **Create Expression** dialog box appears.

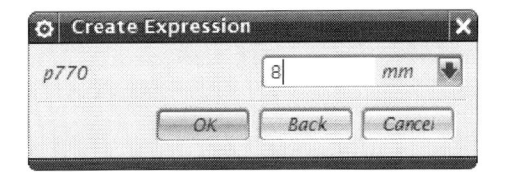

13. Enter -8 mm in the dialog box.

14. Click **OK** twice to create the slot feature.

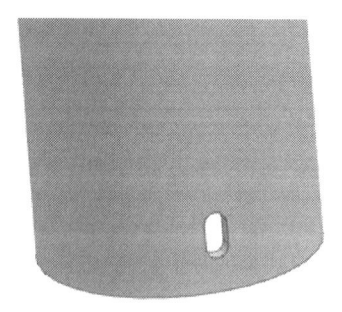

15. Click **Cancel** to exit the tool.

Creating the Linear pattern

1. Click **Pattern Feature** on the **Feature** toolbar, or click **Insert > Associate Copy > Pattern Feature**; the **Pattern Feature** dialog box appears.

2. Select **Linear** from the **Layout** drop-down list.

3. Select the slot feature.

4. Click **Specify Vector** in the **Direction 1** group; a triad appears.

5. Select Z-axis from the triad.

6. Select **Count and Pitch** from the **Spacing** drop-down.

7. Enter **6** in the **Count** edit box.

8. Enter **16** in the **Pitch Distance** edit box.

9. Click **OK** to create the linear pattern.

Additional Modeling Tools

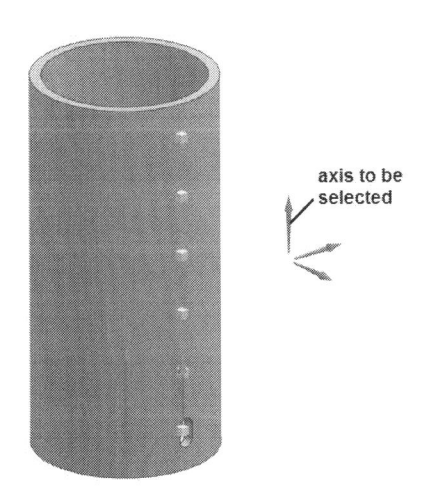

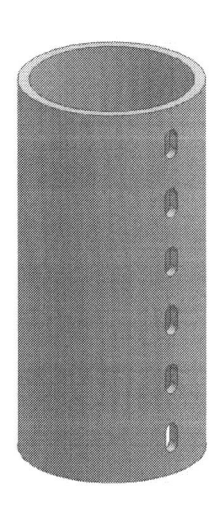

Creating the Circular pattern

1. Click **Pattern Feature** on the **Feature** toolbar.

2. Select **Circular** from the **Layout** drop-down list.

3. Press Ctrl key and then select the linear pattern and the slot feature from the **Part Navigator**.

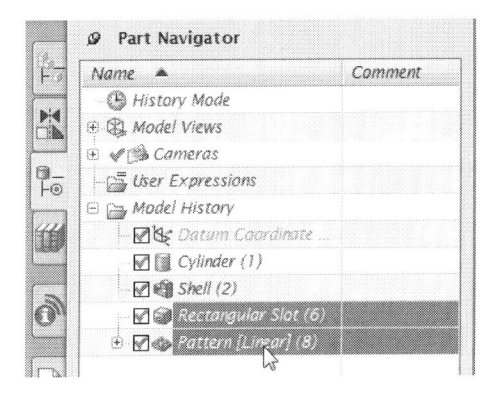

4. Click **Specify Vector** in the **Rotation Axis** group; a triad appears.

5. Select Z-axis from the triad.

   Now, you have to specify the point through which the rotation axis passes.

6. Click on the circular edge of the cylindrical feature (to select the center point of the cylinder).

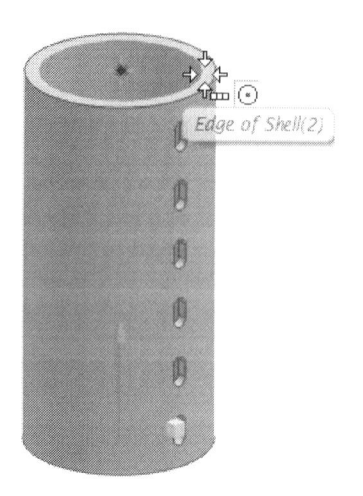

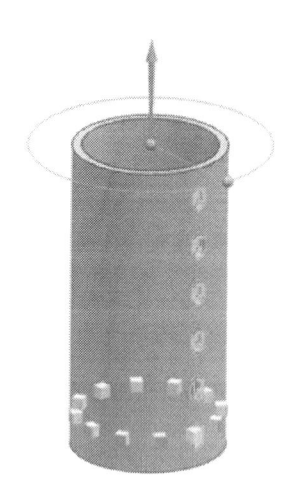

7. Select **Count and Span** from the **Spacing** drop-down.

8. Enter **12** in the **Count** edit box.

9. Enter **360** in the **Span Angle** edit box.

10. Click **OK** to create the circular pattern.

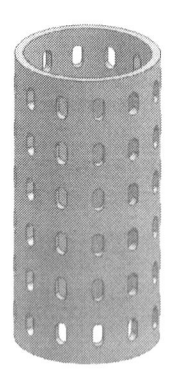

11. Save and close the model.

TUTORIAL 5
In this tutorial, you will create a chain.

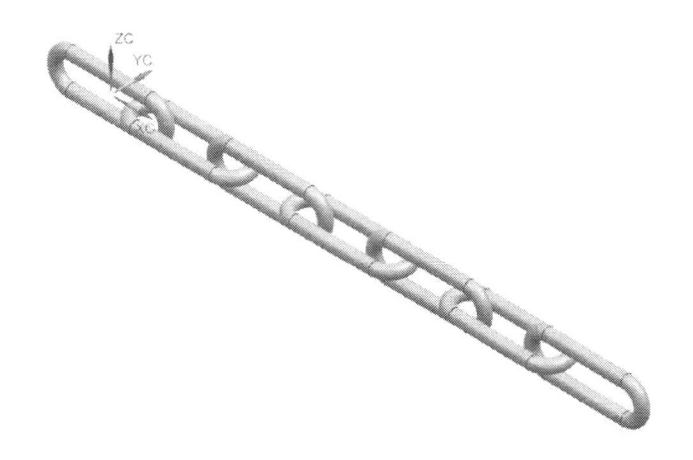

Open a new part file creating the Tube feature

1. Open a new file using the **Model** template.

2. Click **Sketch** on the **Direct Sketch** toolbar.

3. Select the XZ plane.

4. Click **Rectangle** on the **Direct Sketch** toolbar; the **Rectangle** dialog bar appears.

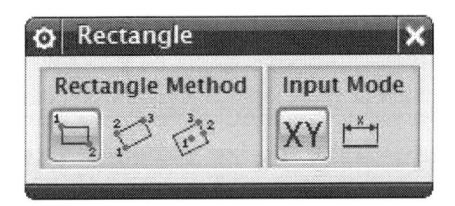

5. Click **From Center** on the dialog bar.

6. Select the origin point.

7. Create the rectangle.

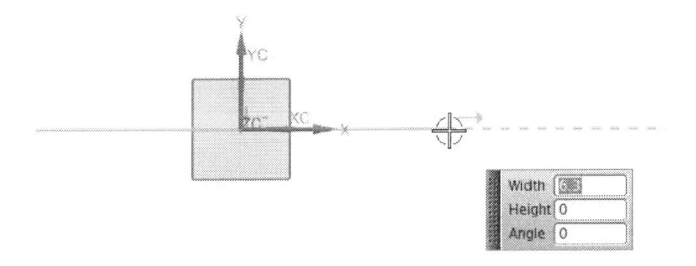

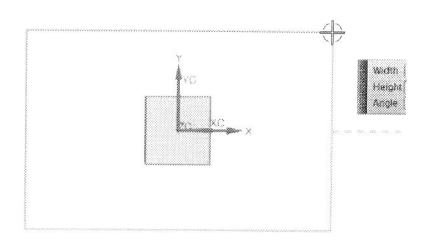

8. Dimension the rectangle.

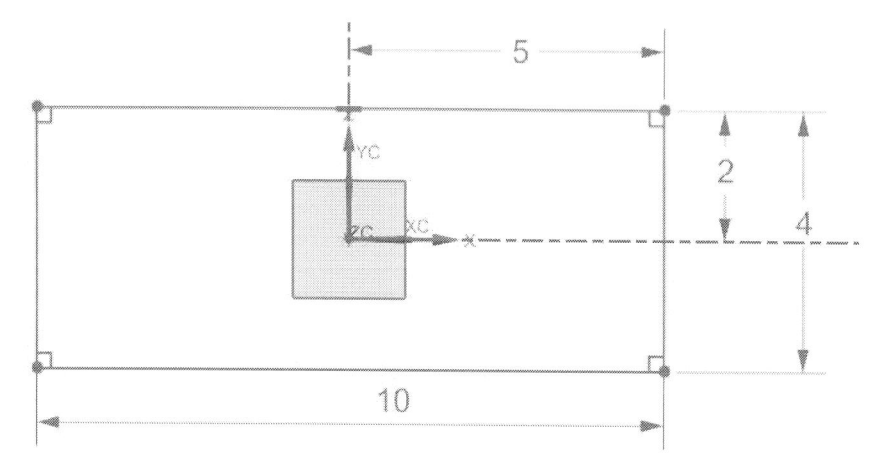

9. Create a circle.

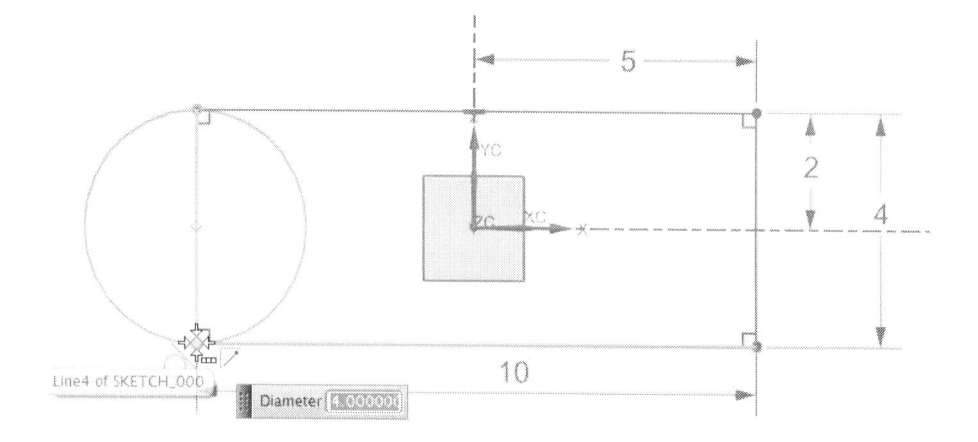

10. Click **Mirror Curve** from the **Curve from Curves** drop-down on the **Direct Sketch** toolbar.

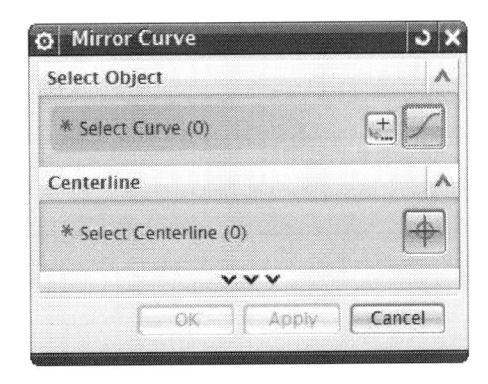

11. Select the circle from the sketch.

12. Click **Select Centerline** on the **Mirror Curve** dialog box.

13. Select the vertical axis from the origin.

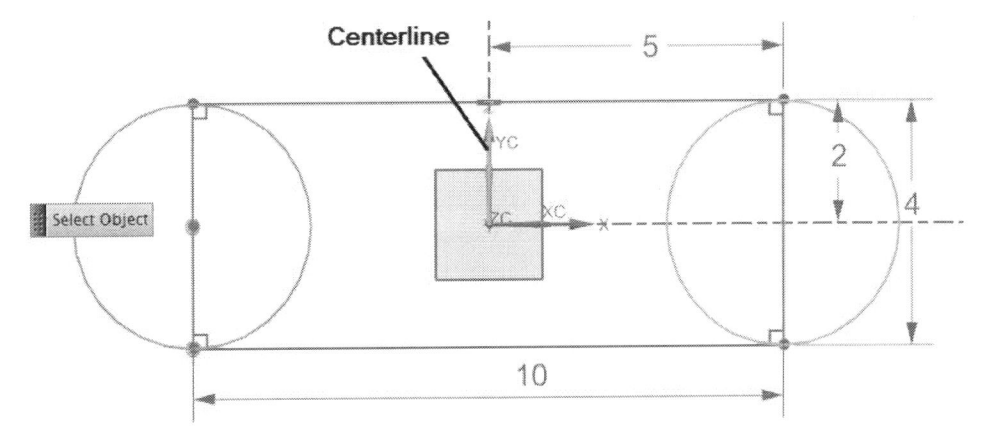

14. Click **OK** to create the mirror curve.

15. Click **Quick Trim** button on the **Direct Sketch** toolbar.

16. Trim the unwanted entities.

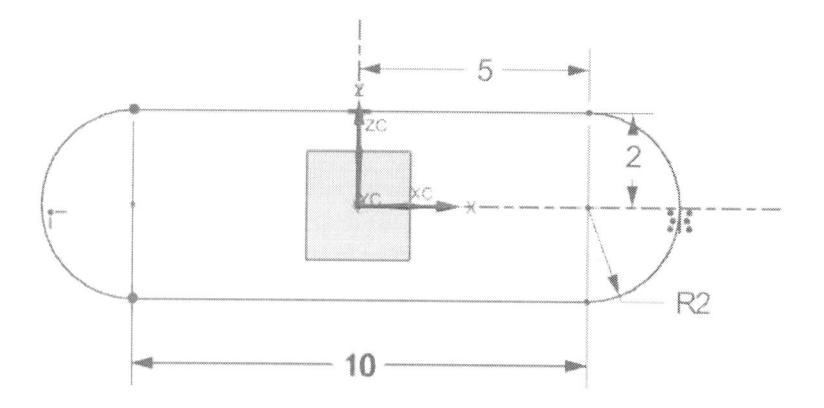

17. Click **Finish Sketch** on the **Direct Sketch** toolbar.

18. To create a tube feature, click **Insert > Sweep > Tube** from the menu bar; the **Tube** dialog box appears.

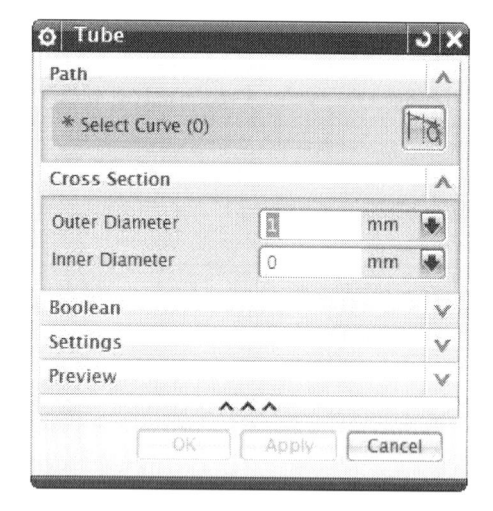

19. Select the sketch.

20. Enter 1.5 mm and 0 in the **Outer Diameter** and **Inner Diameter** edit boxes, respectively.

21. Click OK to create the tube feature.

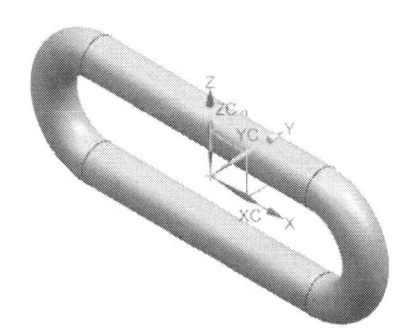

Creating the Instances of the Tube feature

1. To create the instances, click **Instance Geometry** button on the **Feature** toolbar, or click **Insert > Associate Copy > Instance Geometry** on the menu bar; the **Instance Geometry** dialog box appears.

2. Select **Rotate** from the **Type** drop-down.

3. Select the tube feature.

4. Click **Specify Vector** in the **Rotation Axis** group.

5. Select the X-axis of the traid.

6. Select the origin point of the coordinate system.

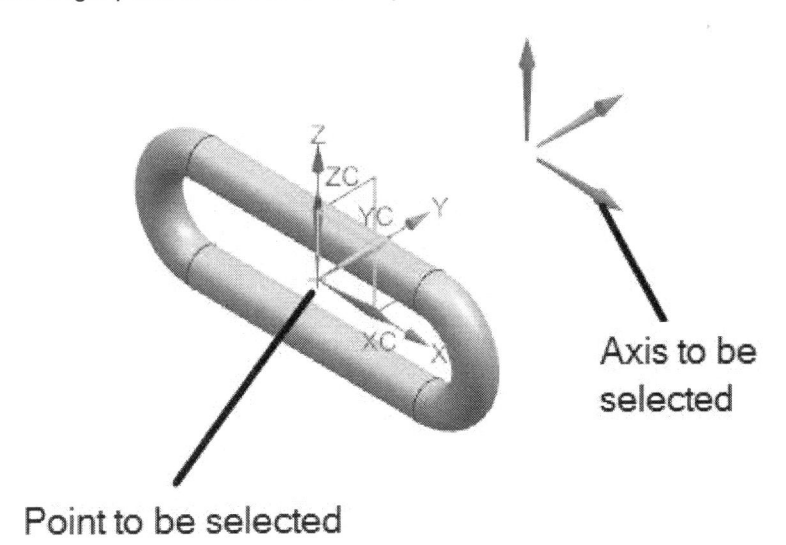

Axis to be selected

Point to be selected

7. Specify **Angle** as 90 degrees.

   Distance = 10 mm

   Number of Copies = 6

8. Click **OK** to create instances of the tube.

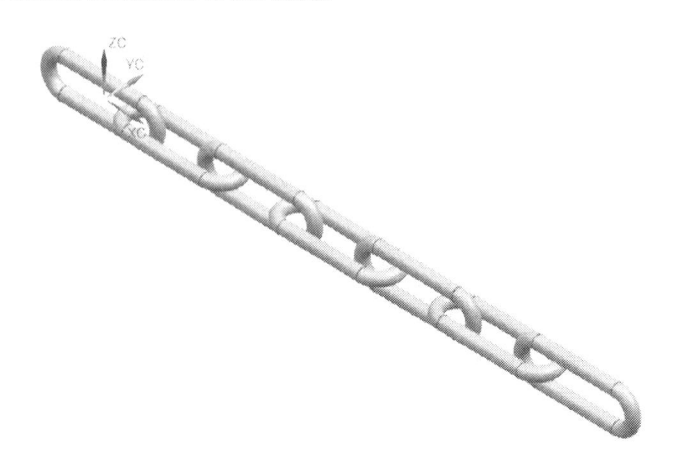

9. Save and close the file.

Boolean Operations

Types of boolean operations.

- Unite
- Subtract
- Intersect

These tools are used to combine, subtract, or Intersect two bodies. You can invoke these tools from the **Combine** drop-down on the **Feature** toolbar or from the menu bar (go to **Insert > Combine**)

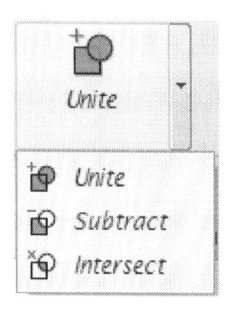

Unite: This tool is used to combine the **Tool Body** and the **Target Body** into a single body.

Subtract: This tool is used to subtract the **Tool body** from the **Target body**.

Intersect: This tool is used to keep the intersecting portion of the tool and target bodies.

TUTORIAL 6

In this tutorial, you will create the model shown in figure.

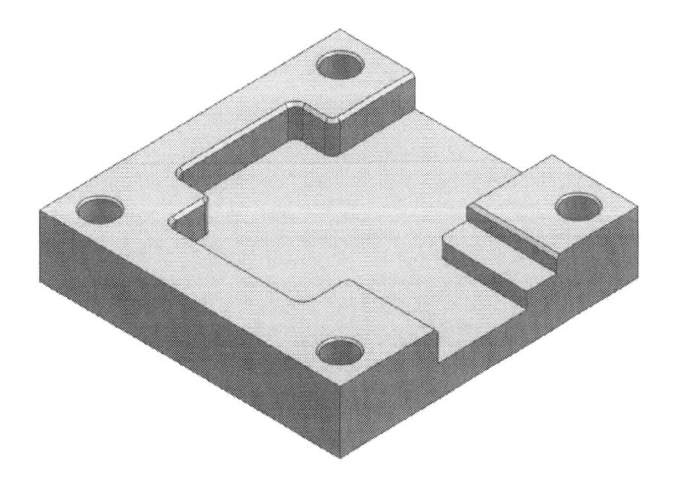

Creating the Base feature

1. Create the base feature on the XY plane (extrude the sketch upto a distance of 40 mm).

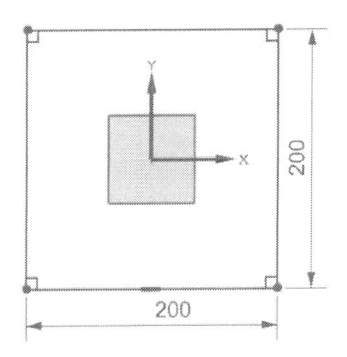

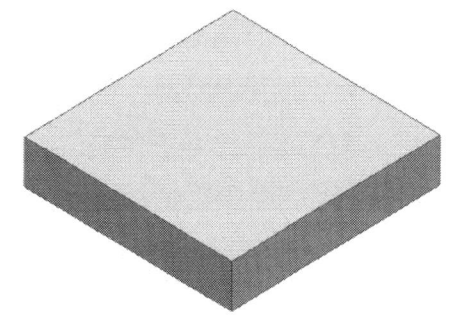

Creating the Cut Feature

1. Create the sketch on the top face of the base feature.

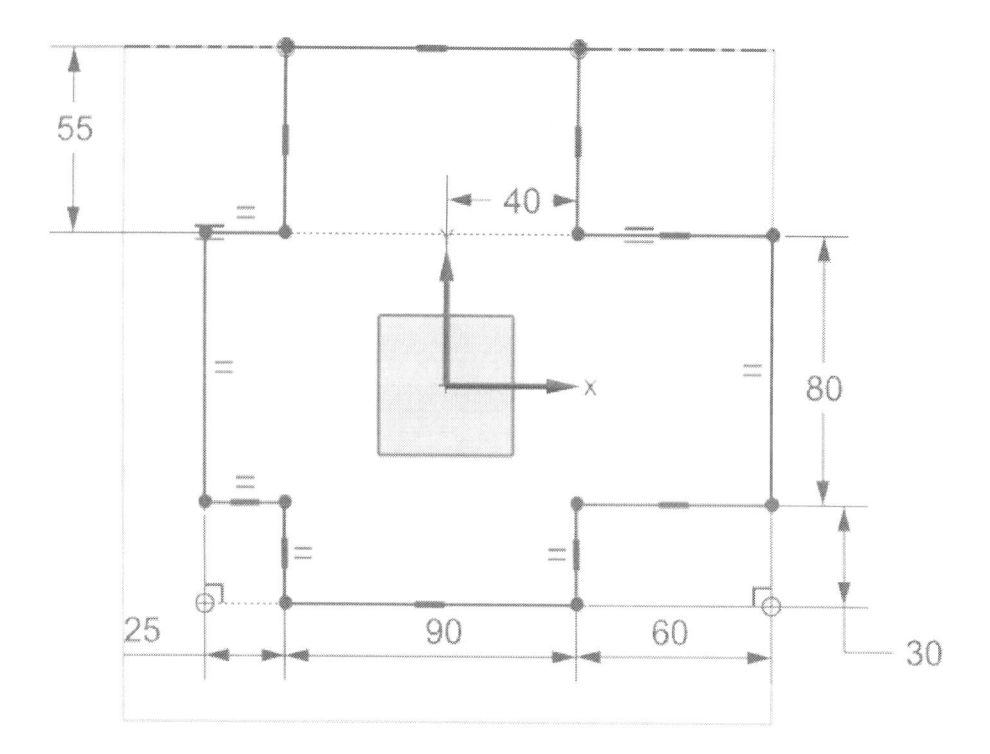

2. Click the **Extrude** button on the **Feature** toolbar.

3. Select the sketch.

4. Enter **20** in the **Distance** edit box below the **End** drop-down.

5. Select **Subtract** from the **Boolean** drop-down.

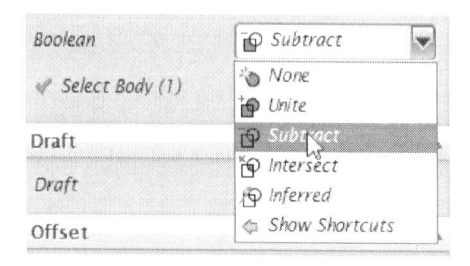

6. Click the **Reverse Direction** button in the **Direction** group.

7. Click **OK** to create the cut feature.

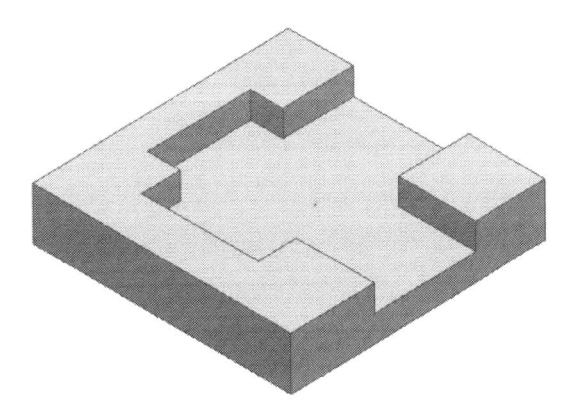

Creating the third feature

1. Create the sketch on the face created by the cut feature.

2. Click the **Extrude** button on the **Feature** toolbar.

3. Select the sketch.

4. Enter **10** in the **Distance** edit box below the **End** drop-down list.

5. Select **Unite** from the **Boolean** drop-down.

6. Click OK.

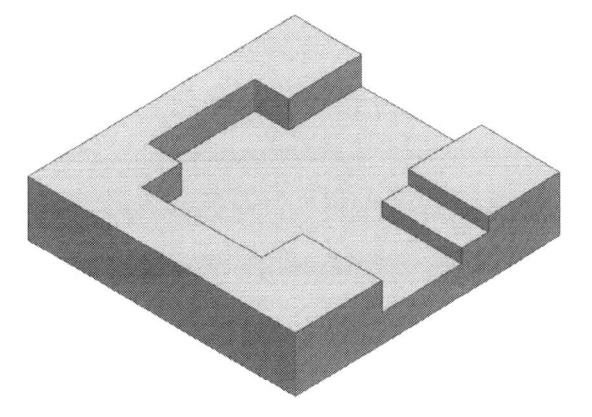

Creating Holes

1. To create holes, click **Hole** on the **Feature** toolbar, or click **Insert > Design Feature > Hole** on the menu bar; the **Hole** dialog box appears.

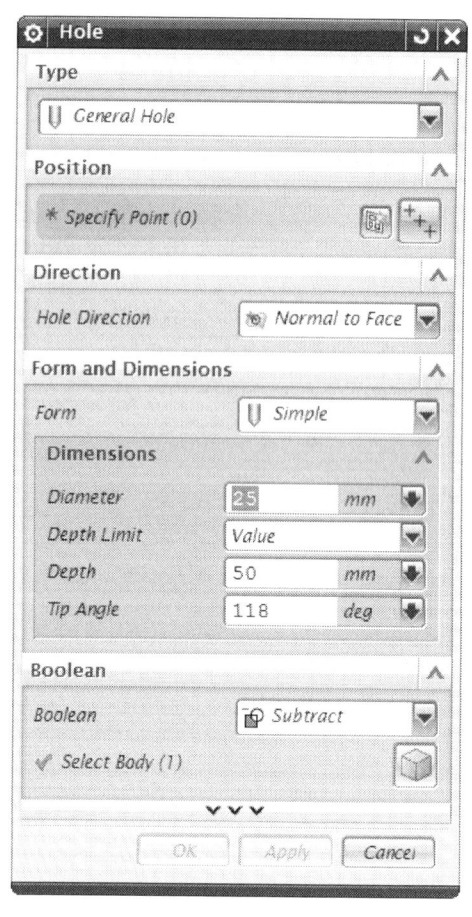

2. Select **Drill Size Hole** from the **Type** drop-down.

3. Click on the top face of the model.

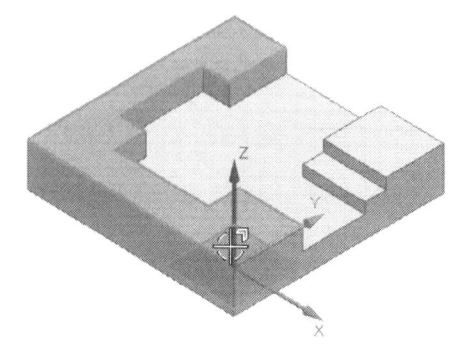

4. Click **Close** on the **Sketch Point** dialog box.

5. Add dimensions to specify the hole location.

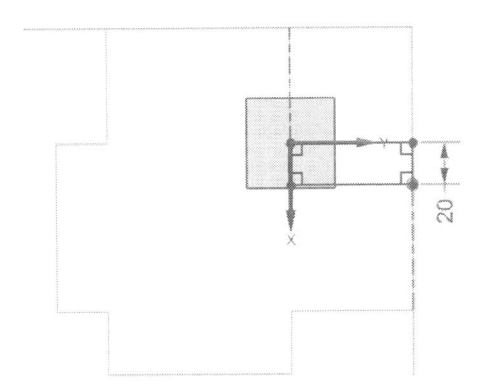

6. Click **Finish Sketch**.

7. Select **20** from the **Size** drop-down in the **Forms and Dimensions** group.

8. Click **OK** to create the hole.

Creating Patterns of the holes

1. Click **Pattern Feature** on the **Feature** toolbar.

2. Select the hole.

3. Select **Linear** from the **Layout** drop-down.

4. Click **Specify Vector** in the **Direction 1** group; a triad appears.

5. Select Y-axis from the triad.

6. Select **Count and Span** from the **Spacing** drop-down.

7. Enter **2** in the **Count** edit box.

8. Enter **160** in the **Span Distance** edit box.

9. Select **Use Direction 2**.

10. Select X-axis from the triad.

11. Select **Count and Span** from the **Spacing** drop-down.

12. Specify the same values (2 and 160) for **Count** and **Span Distance**.

13. Click **Reverse Direction** button.

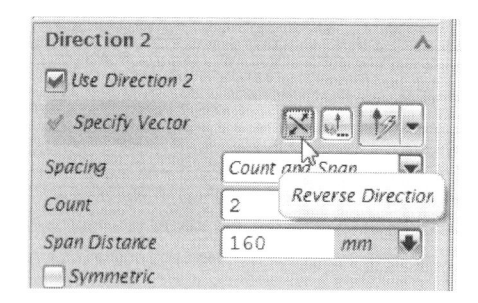

14. Click **OK** to create the linear pattern.

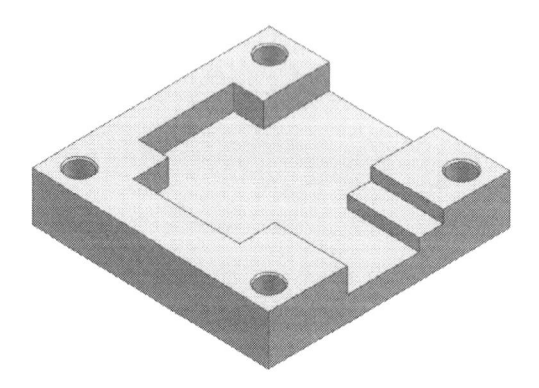

Creating Edge blends
1. Apply edge blends of radius 5 mm.

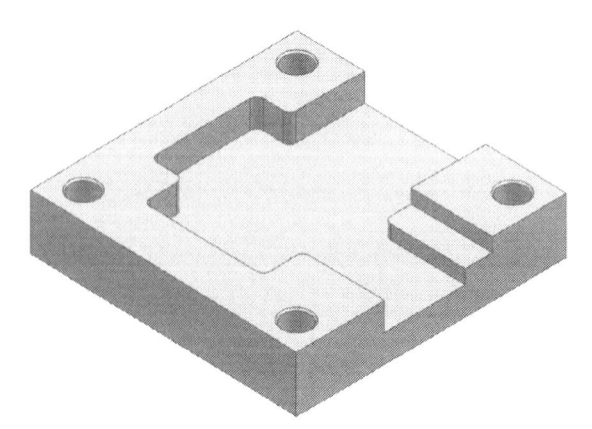

Creating Chamfer
1. To create chamfer, click **Chamfer** on the **Feature** toolbar, or click **Insert > Detail Feature > Chamfer** on the menu bar; the **Chamfer** dialog box appears.

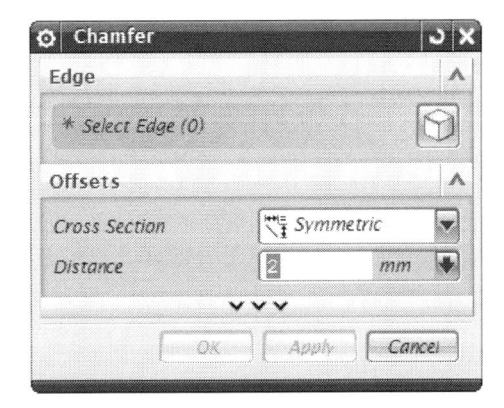

2. Select the edges on the top face of the model.

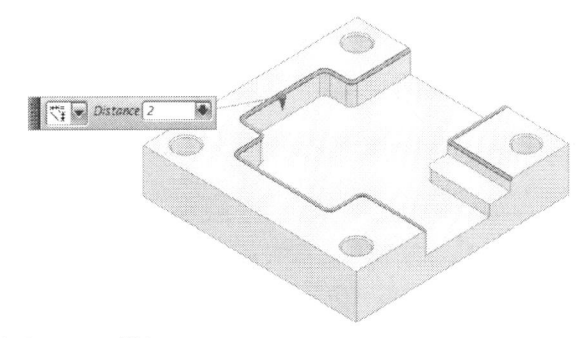

3. Enter **2** in the **Distance** edit box.

4. Click **OK** to create the chamfers.

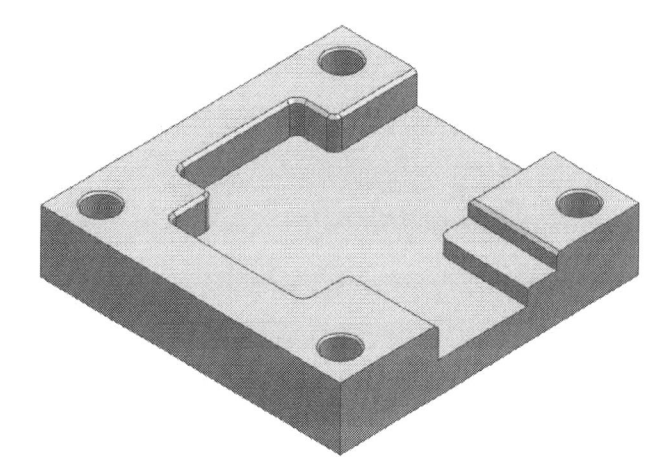

5. Save the model with the name **Tutorial 6**.

6. Close the file.

6

Sheet metal Modeling

This Chapter will show you to:

- Create Tab feature
- Create Flange
- Contour Flange
- Closed corners
- Louvers
- Beads
- Drawn Cutouts
- Gussets
- Flat Pattern

TUTORIAL 1

In this tutorial, you create the sheet metal model shown in figure.

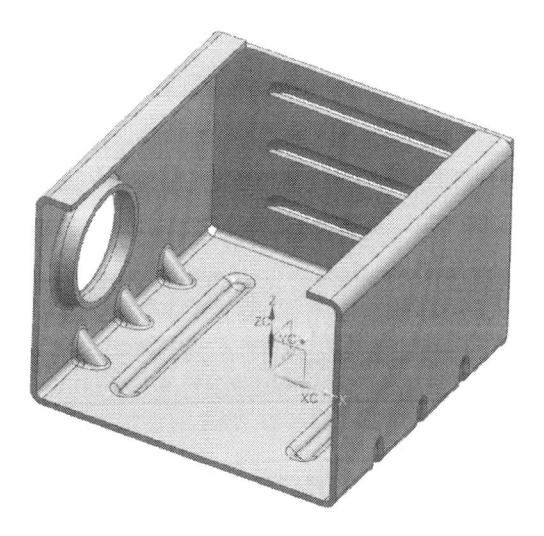

Creating a New Sheet metal File

1. To create a new sheet metal file, click the **New** button on the **Standard** toolbar, or click **File > New** on the menu bar; the **New** dialog box appears.

2. Click **NX Sheet Metal** in the **Template** group.

3. Click **OK**; a new NX Sheet metal window appears.

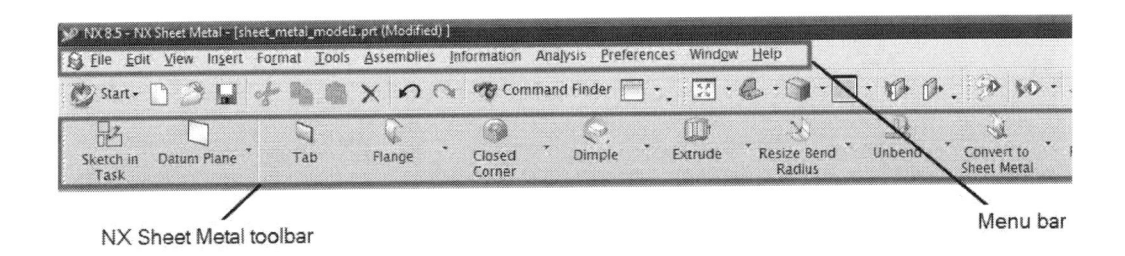

Setting the Parameters of the Sheet Metal part

1. To set the parameters, click **Preferences > NX Sheet Metal** on the menu bar; the **NX Sheet Metal Preferences** dialog box appears.

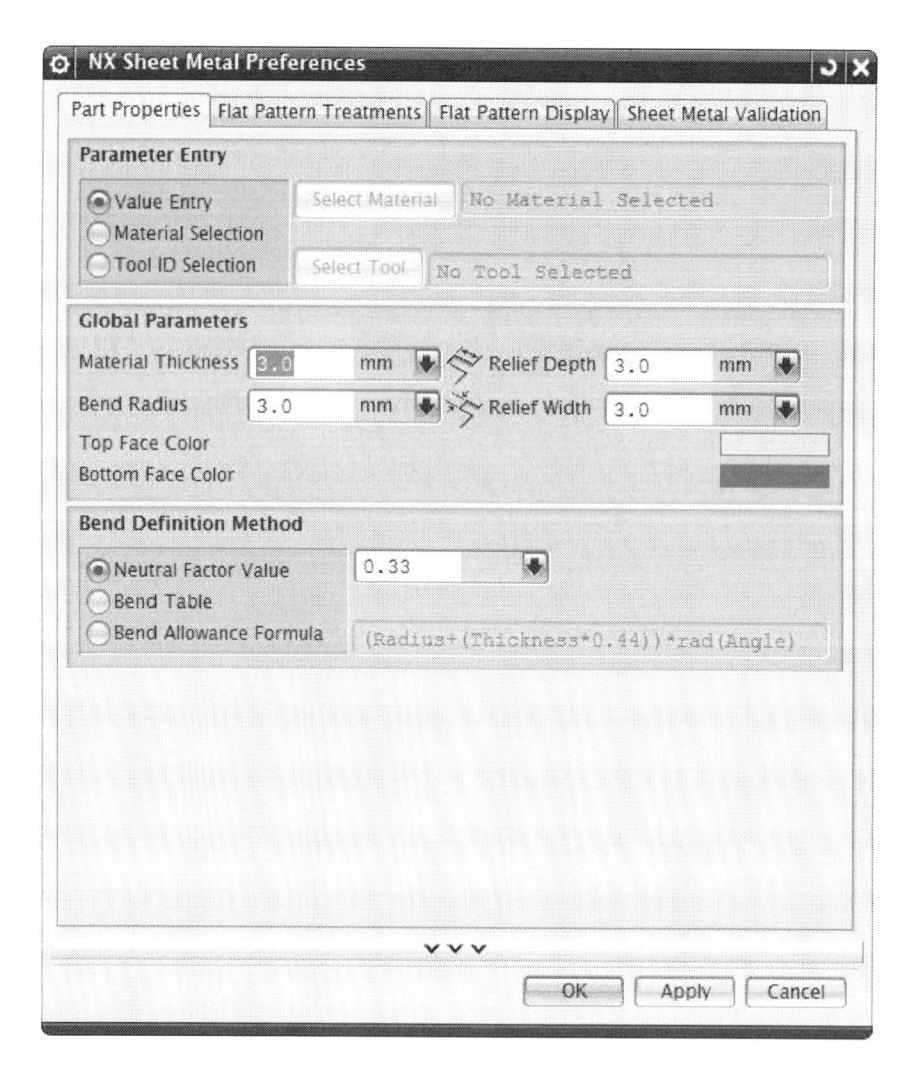

In this dialog box, you can specify the preferences of the sheet metal part such as thickness, bend radius, relief depth, width and so on. In this tutorial, you will create the sheet metal part with the default preferences.

Creating the Base Feature
1. To create the base feature, click **Tab** on the **NX Sheet Metal** toolbar, or click **Insert > Tab** on the menu bar; the **Tab** dialog box appears.

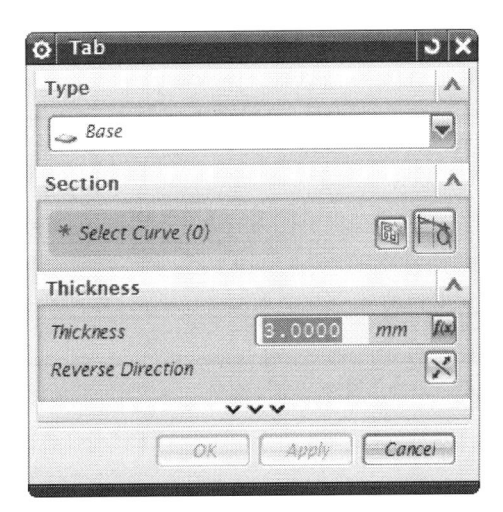

2. Select the XY plane from the coordinate system.

3. Create the sketch as shown in figure.

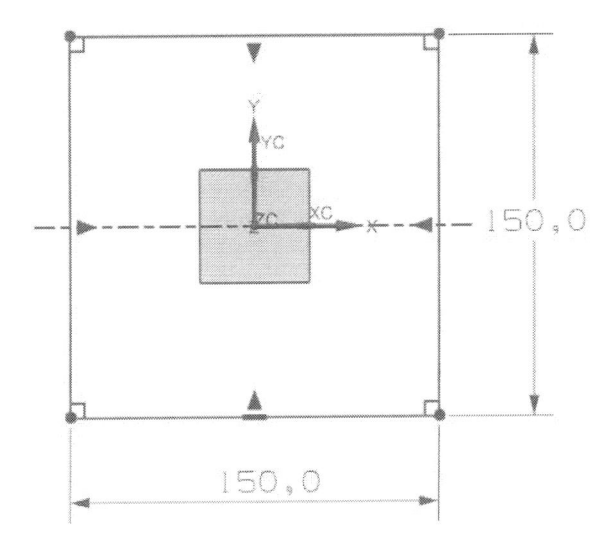

4. Click **Finish Sketch**.

5. Click **OK** to create the tab feature.

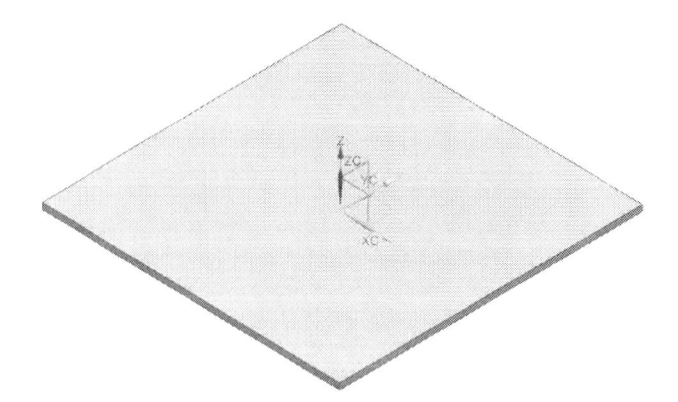

Creating the flange

1. To create the flange, click the **Flange** button on the **NX Sheet Metal** toolbar, or click **Insert > Bend > Flange** on the menu bar; the **Flange** dialog box appears.

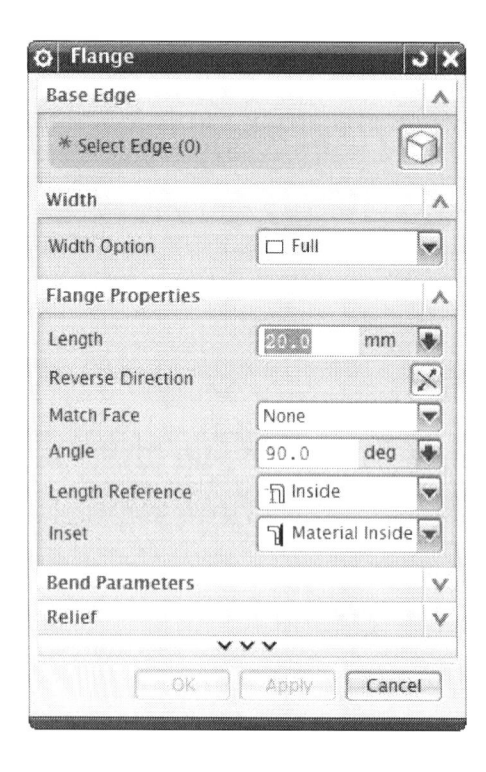

2. Select the edge on the top face.

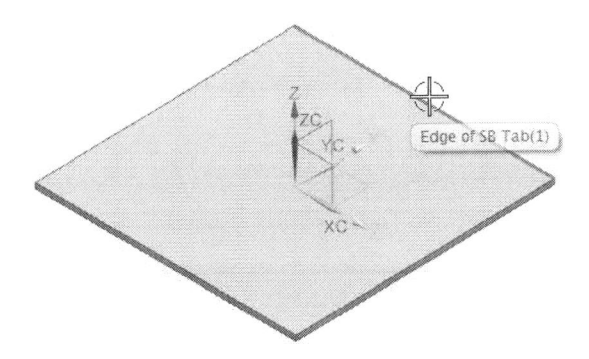

3. Set the **Length** as 100.

4. Click **OK** to create the flange.

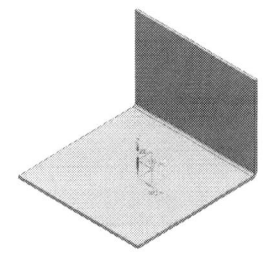

Creating the Contour Flange

1. To create the contour flange, click **Contour Flange** on the **NX Sheet Metal** toolbar, or click **Insert > Bend > Contour Flange** on the menu bar; the **Contour Flange** dialog box appears.

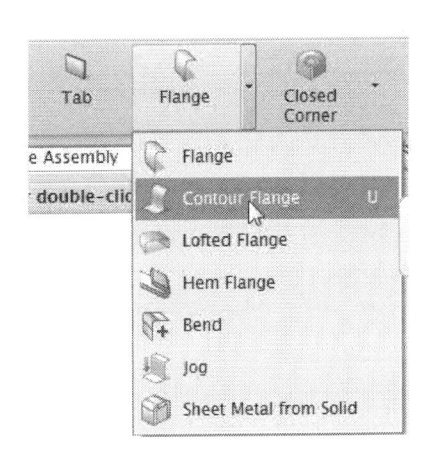

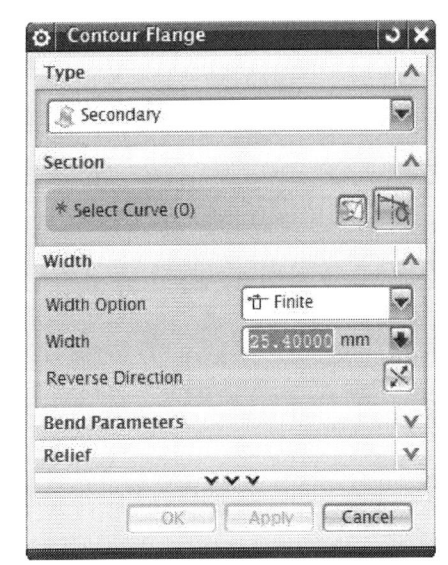

2. Select the edge on the left side of the top face.

3. Enter **100** in the **% Arc Length** edit box in the **Plane Location** group.

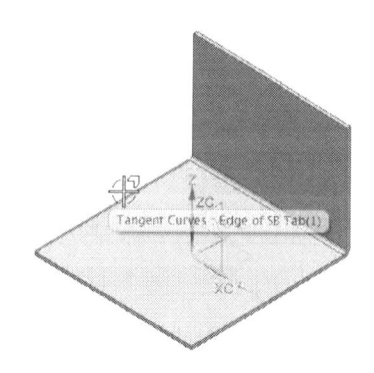

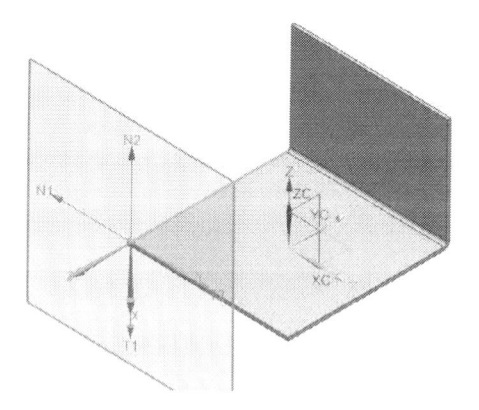

4. Click OK.

5. Draw the sketch, as shown in figure.

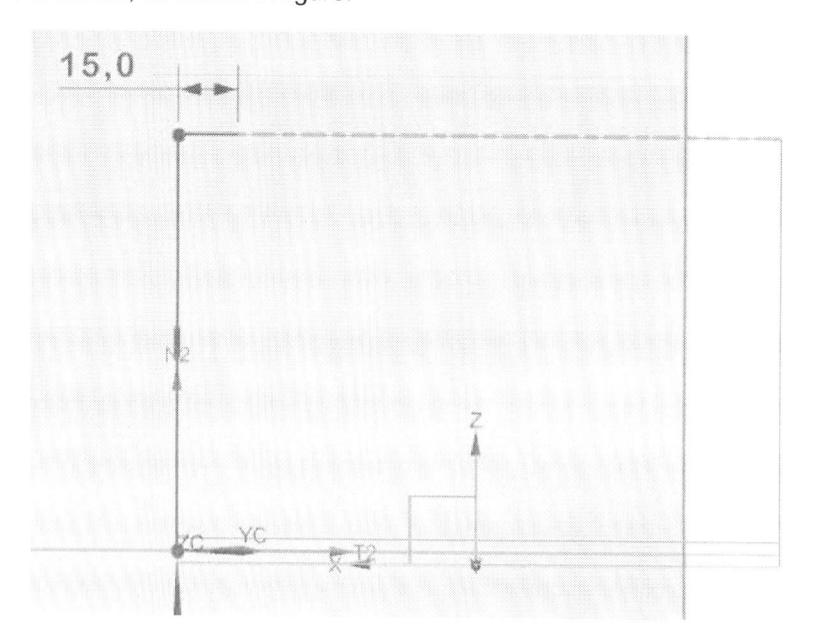

6. Click **Finish Sketch**.

7. Select **To End** from the **Width Option** drop-down.

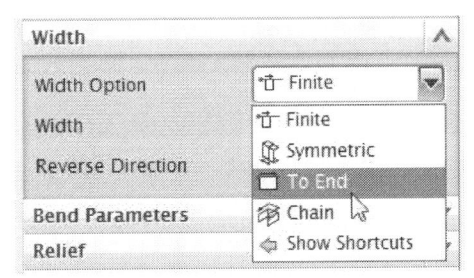

8. Click **OK** to create the contour flange.

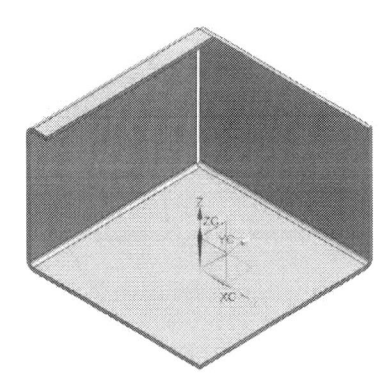

Creating the Closed Corner

1. To create the closed corner, click **Closed Corner** on the **NX Sheet Metal** toolbar, or click **Insert > Corner > Closed Corner** on the menu bar; the **Closed Corner** dialog box appears.

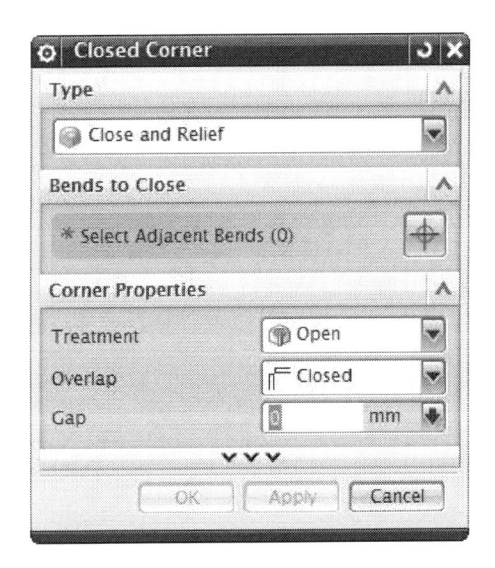

2. Rotate the model (press the middle mouse button and drag the cursor).

3. Select the two bends forming the corner.

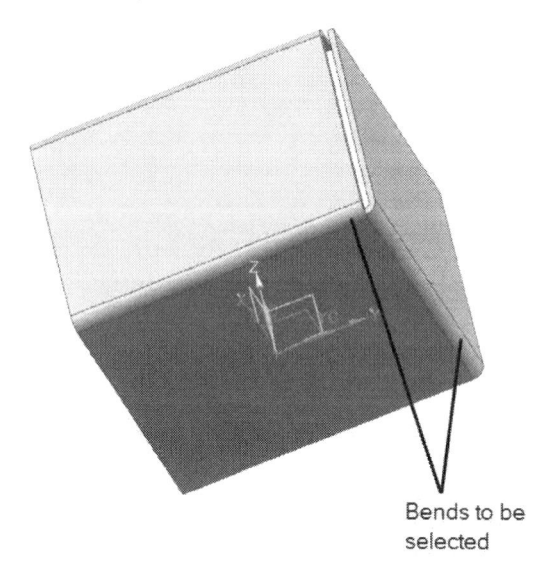

Bends to be selected

4. Select **Open** from the **Treatments** drop-down.

5. Click OK to create the open corner.

You can also apply corner treatment using the options in the **Treatments** drop-down. The different types of the corner treatments are given next.

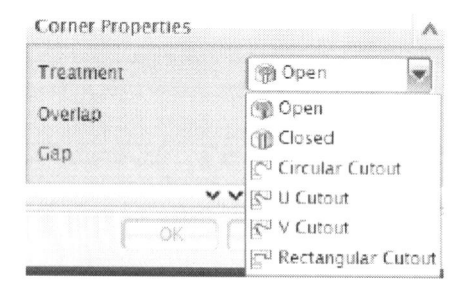

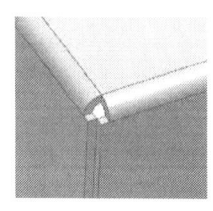

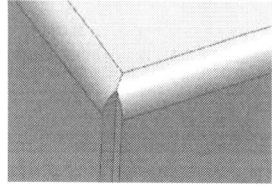

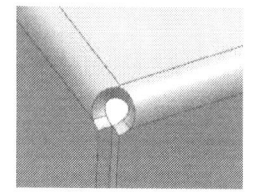

Open   Closed   Circular Cutout

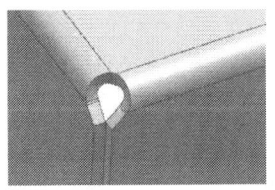

U Cutout 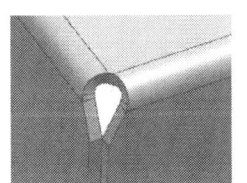   V Cutout 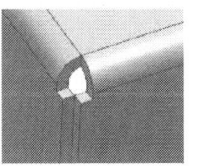   Rectangular Cutout

Creating the Louver

1. To create the louver, click **Louver** on the **NX Sheet Metal** toolbar, or click **Insert > Punch > Louver** on the menu bar; the **Louver** dialog box appears.

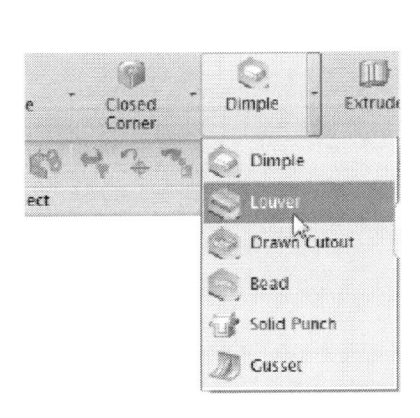

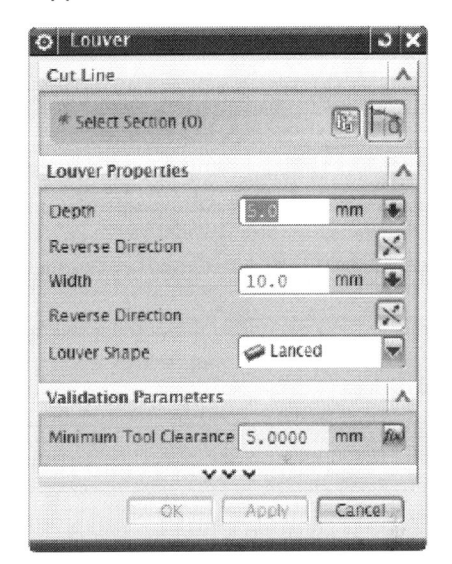

2. Select the front face of the flange.

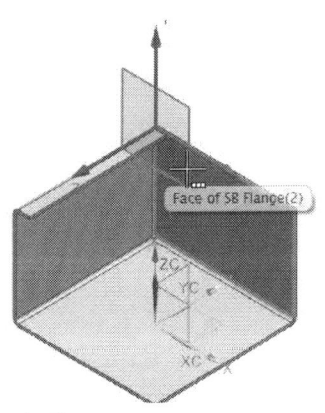

3. Create the sketch as shown in figure.

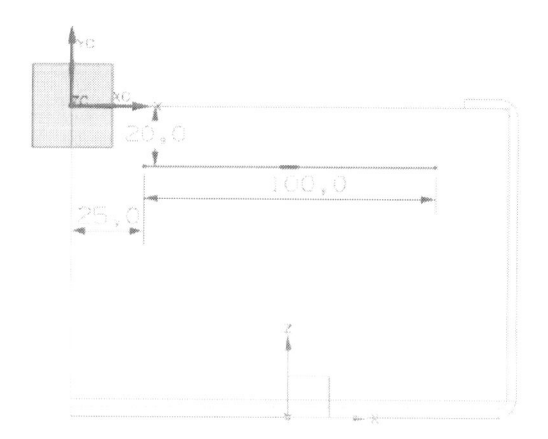

4. Click **Finish Sketch**.

5. Select **Formed** from the **Louver Shape** drop-down.

6. Enter **5** in the **Depth** edit box.

7. Enter **10** in the **Length** edit box.

8. Click the **Reverse Direction** button below the **Depth** edit box.

9. Click the **Reverse Direction** button below the **Width** edit box.

10. Click **OK** to create the louver.

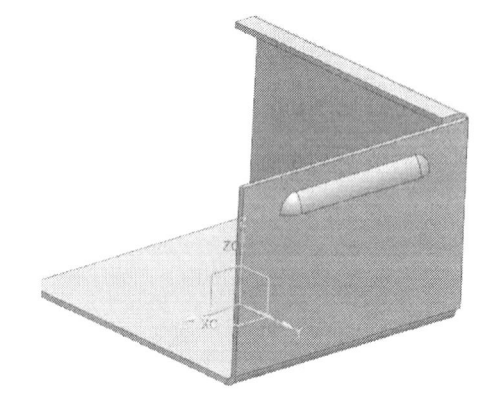

Creating the Pattern Along curve

1. Click **Insert > Associate Copy > Pattern Feature** on the menu bar.

2. Select the louver feature.

3. Select **Along** from the **Layout** drop-down.

4. Click on **Select Path** in the **Direction 1** group.

5. Select the vertical edge of the flange feature.

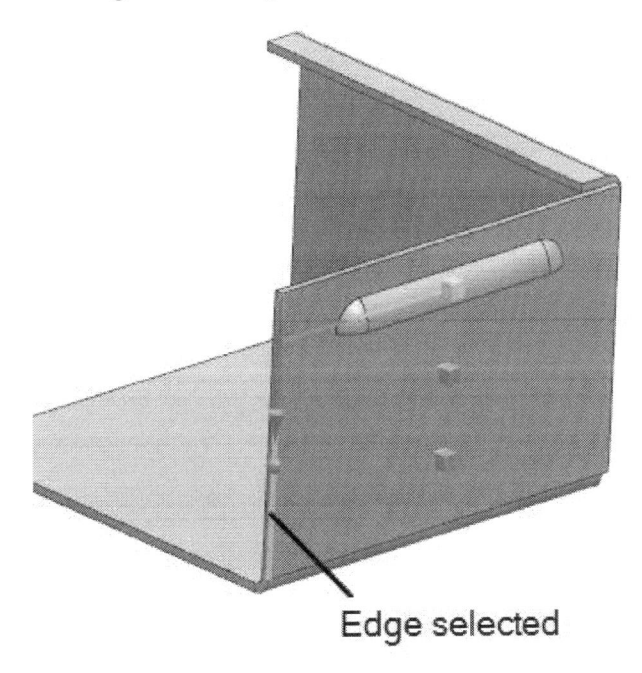

Edge selected

6. Select **Count and Span** from the **Spacing** drop-down.

7. Specify **Count** as 3.

8. Specify **%Span By** as 60.

9. Click **OK** to create the pattern along curve.

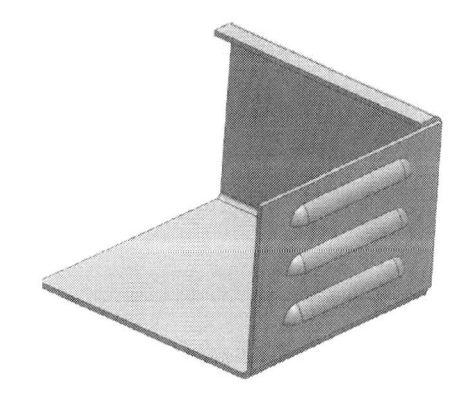

Creating the Bead

1. To create the bead, click **Dimple drop-down >Bead** button on the **NX Sheet Metal** toolbar, or click **Insert > Punch > Bead** on the menu bar; the **Bead** dialog box appears.

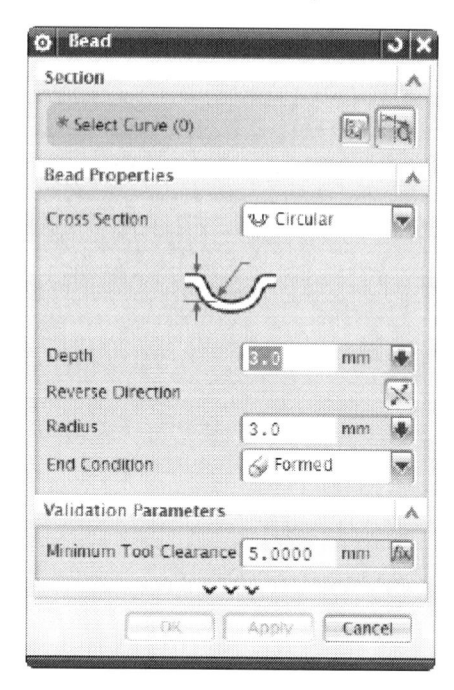

2. Select the top face of the base feature.

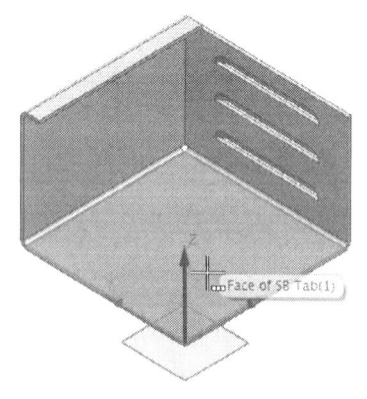

3. Create the sketch as shown in figure.

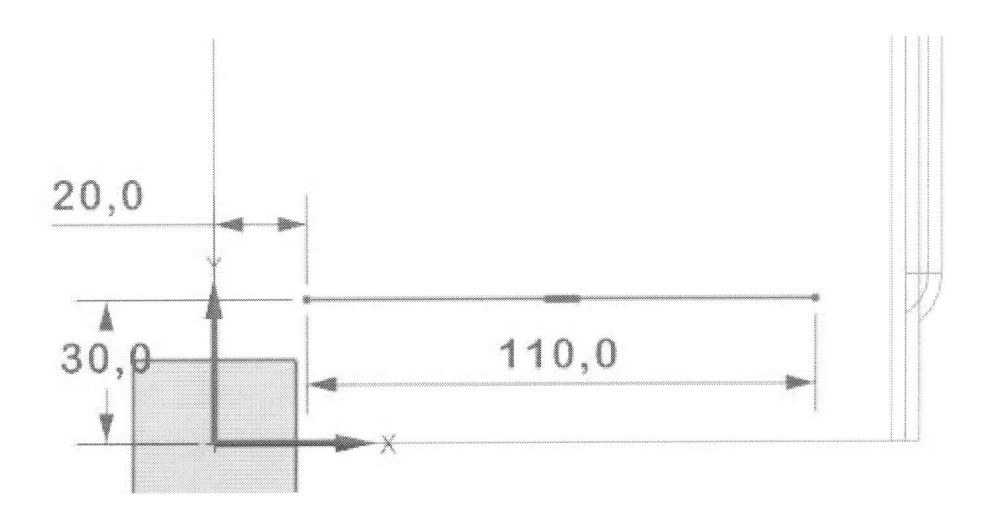

4. Click **Finish Sketch**.

5. Select **Circular** from the **Cross Section** drop-down.

6. Set **Depth** as 4.

7. Set **Radius** as 4.

8. Click **Reverse Direction** below the **Depth** edit box.

9. Select **Formed** from the **End Condition** drop-down.

10. Click **OK** to create the bead.

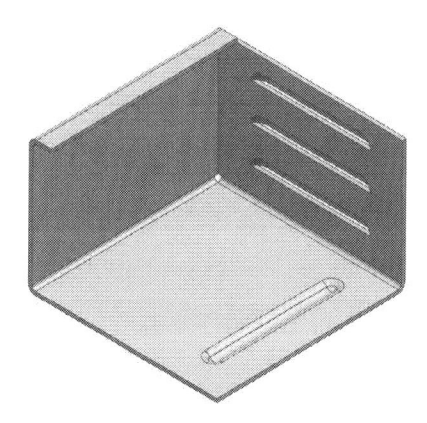

Creating the Drawn Cutout

1. To create the drawn cutout, click **Dimple drop-down > Drawn Cutout** button on the **NX Sheet Metal** toolbar, or click **Insert > Punch > Drawn Cutout** on the menu bar; the **Drawn Cutout** dialog box appears.

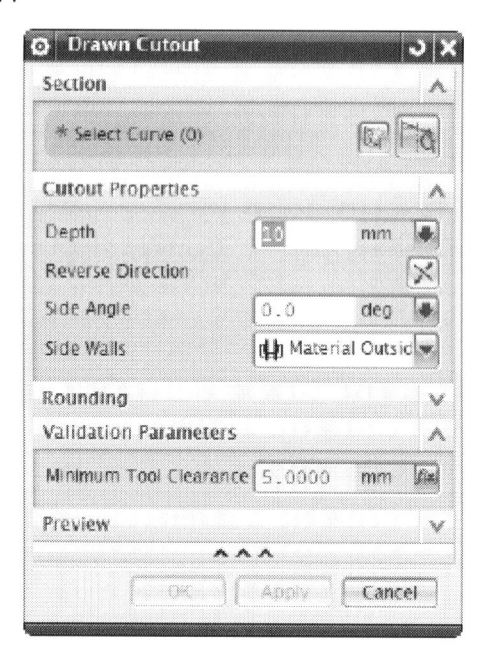

2. Select the face of the contour flange.

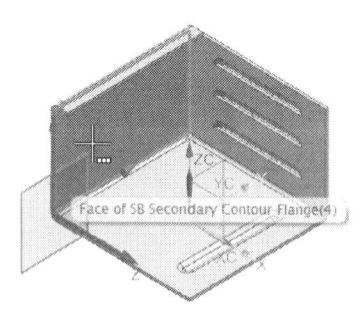

3. Draw the sketch as shown in figure.

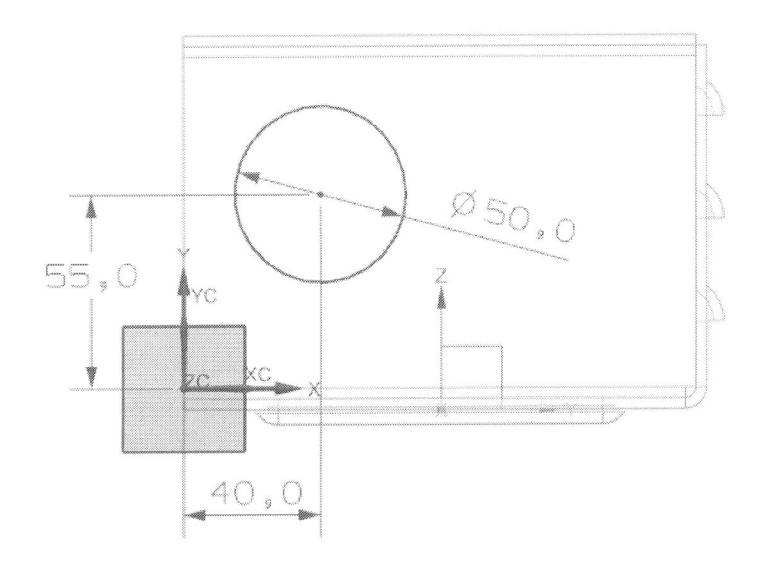

4. Click **Finish Sketch**.

5. Set **Depth** as 10.

6. Set **Side Angle** as 5.

7. Clear the **Round Section Corners** check box in **Rounding** group.

8. Set **Die Radius** as 3.

9. Click **OK** to create the drawn cutout.

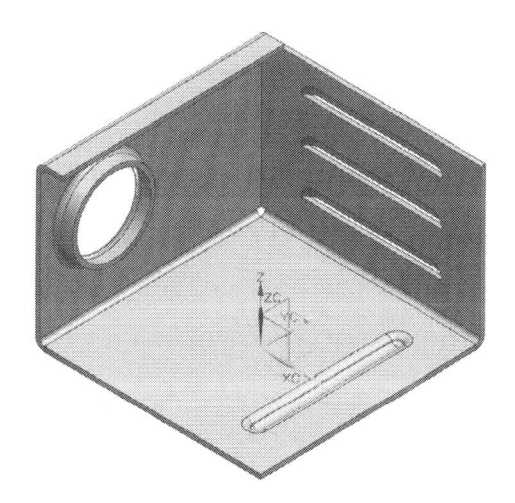

Creating Gussets

1. To create gussets, click **Dimple drop-down > Gusset** button on the **NX Sheet Metal** toolbar, or click **Insert > Punch > Gusset** on the menu bar; the **Gusset** dialog box appears.

2. Select the bend face of the contour flange.

3. Select **Fit** from the **Placement** drop-down.

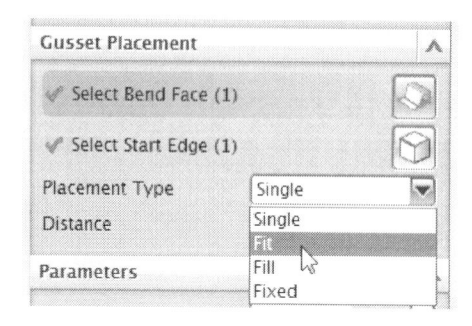

4. Specify **Count** as 3.

5. Specify **Depth** as 12.

6. Select **Round** from the **Shape** drop-down.

7. Set **Width** as 10.

8. Set **Side Angle** as 2.

9. Set **Punch Radius** and **Die Radius** as 2.

10. Click **OK** to create gussets.

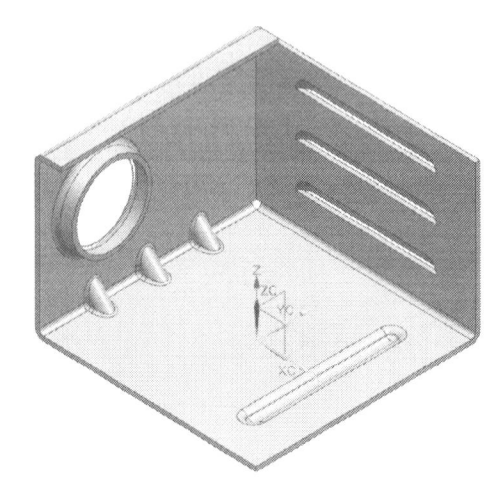

Creating the Mirror Feature

1. To create the mirror feature, click **Insert > Associate Copy > Mirror Feature** on the menu bar; the **Mirror Feature** dialog box appears.

2. Press Ctrl key and then select the contour flange, closed corner, bead feature, and gusset from the **Part Navigator**.

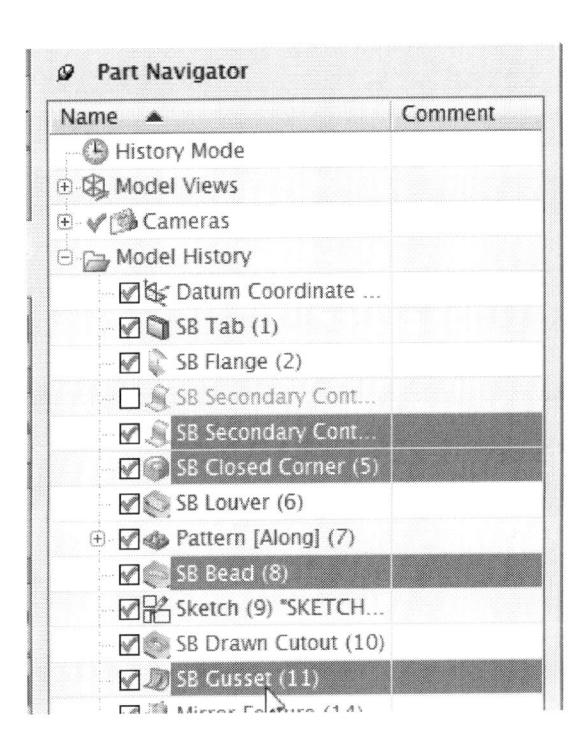

3. Click on **Select Plane** in the **Mirror Plane** group.

4. Select the YZ plane from the coordinate system.

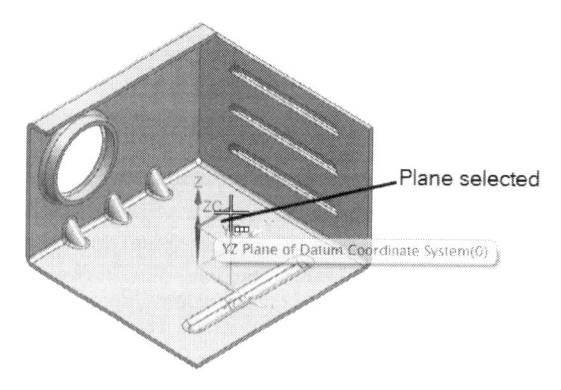

5. Click **OK** to create the mirror feature.

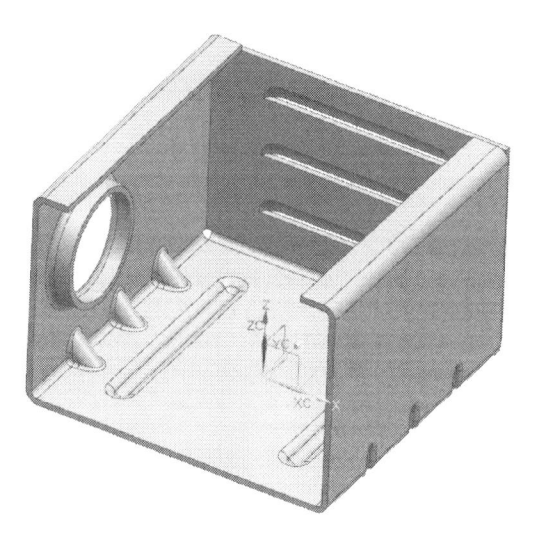

Creating the Flat Pattern

1. To create the flat pattern, click **Flat Pattern drop-down > Flat Pattern** button on the **NX Sheet Metal** toolbar, or click **Insert > Flat Pattern > Flat Pattern** on the menu bar; the **Flat Pattern** dialog box appears.

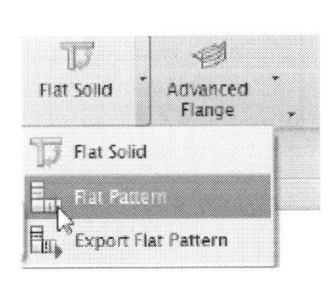

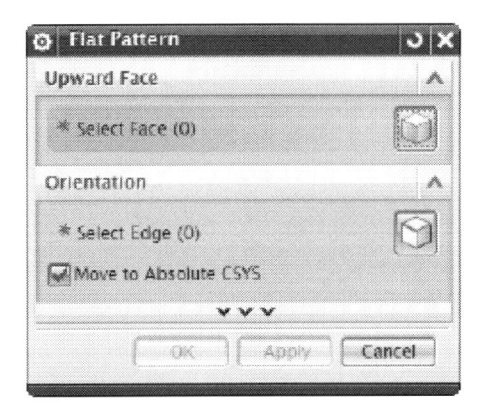

2. Select the top face of the base feature.

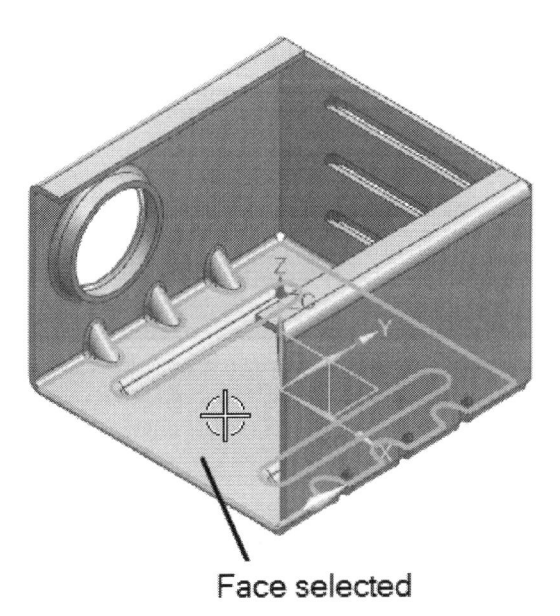

Face selected

3. Clear the **Move to Absolute CSYS** check box.

4. Click **OK** to create the flat pattern.

5. To view the flat pattern, click **View > Layout > Replace View** from the menu bar; the **Replace View with** dialog box appears.

6. Select the FLAT-PATTERN from the dialog box.

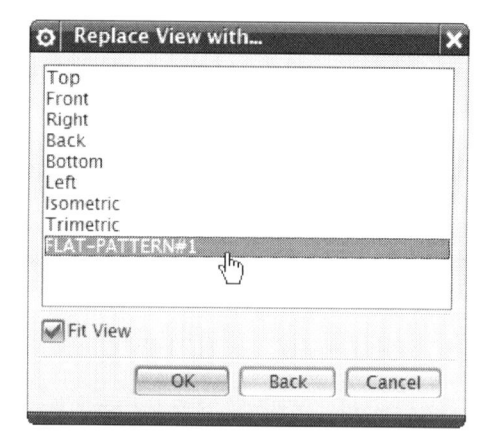

7. Click **OK** to display the flat pattern.

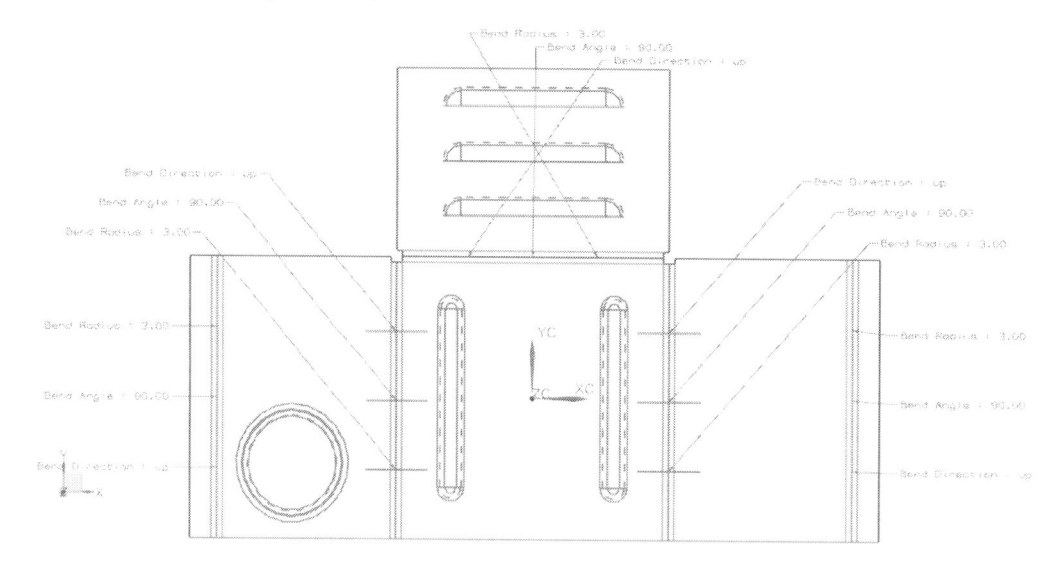

8. Save and close the file.

Made in the USA
Lexington, KY
05 September 2013